KLONDIKE JOE BOYLE

KLONDIKE JOE BOYLE

Heroic Adventures From Gold Fields to Battlefields

HISTORY/BIOGRAPHY

by Stan Sauerwein

PUBLISHED BY ALTITUDE PUBLISHING CANADA LTD.
1500 Railway Avenue, Canmore, Alberta T1W 1P6
www.altitudepublishing.com
1-800-957-6888

Publisher	Stephen Hutchings
Associate Publisher	Kara Turner
Editors	Colleen Anderson, Kara Turner, and Jill Foran

We acknowledge the financial support of the Government
of Canada through the Book Publishing Industry Development
Program (BPIDP) for our publishing activities.

Altitude GreenTree Program
Altitude Publishing will plant twice as many trees as were used
in the manufacturing of this product.

National Library of Canada Cataloguing in Publication Data

Sauerwein, Stan
Klondike Joe Boyle / Stan Sauerwein

(Amazing stories)
Includes bibliographical references.
ISBN 1-55153-969-1

1. Boyle, Joe, 1863-1923. 2. Adventure and adventurers--Canada--
Biography. 3. Gold miners--Yukon Territory--Biography. 4. Yukon
Territory--Biography. I. Title. II. Series: Amazing stories (Canmore, Alta.)
FC4022.1.B6S28 2003   971.9'102'092   C2003-911127-X

An application for the trademark for Amazing Stories™
has been made and the registered trademark is pending.

Printed and bound in Canada by Friesens
2 4 6 8 9 7 5 3 1

Cover: Lt. Col. Joe Boyle in 1918
Photograph courtesy of Woodstock Museum National Historic Site

Author's note to readers

In drafting this book, I chose to use "Rumania" as the spelling for that country because during
the timescape for this story it was the popular use, though "Romania" was starting to become
more acceptable.

In 1859-61 the principalities of Wallachia and Moldavia were united, and adopted the name
of Rumânia for the new state that supposed their descendency from the Roman colonists in
Dacia. Afterwards the spelling was changed to România. In English both variants, Rumania
and Romania (without the diacritical mark over the *a*), are used, the latter becoming more
popular because it is the officially adopted name of the state.

To the children of great men, who are so often robbed of a father in childhood.

A political map of Europe (in 2003) showing capital
cities and other cities mentioned in the story.

Contents

Prologue

He hefted his yellow haversack and reached for the rope. It hung from the scoured deck of the Susan *in a lazy sag that dipped downwards to a bollard on the dock, more like a tired snake than a handrail. In a large, meaty hand he gripped it for meagre balance, and for the first time since lifting anchor in Ireland he stepped towards land. He didn't look back.*

Joe Whiteside Boyle, barely 20, was a robust 187 pounds and he walked with the bobbing gait of a fighter. He had muscular arms, a chest the size of a rum cask, and piercing blue eyes, but he wasn't a man who lived in the cupped hand of God. When he'd run away to sea at 17, Joe had no way of knowing he was born for solid ground. On one of his marine journeys, he had almost drowned in the rage of an ocean gale when his first ship, a three-masted barque named Wallace, *rounded the Horn. The sight of New York harbour was a welcome blessing to this Ontario horse breeder's son.*

Joe was kind-hearted when it suited him, and that

often depended upon what he received in return. Not that he refused to help a friend when he was called on for a strong hand. Quite the contrary. Joe stepped in when others were afraid to help, but he was a pragmatist. He gave where and when it was warranted, and he took his fair and honourable compensation without guilt. He never demanded more than his due nor accepted less. He'd saved his share of cargo profits like a miser, always planning for the day he'd return home.

With a wave to the city he'd left three years earlier, he stepped towards that future, eager and confident.

Chapter 1
Fighting Irish

Born just four months after Confederation, Joe Whiteside Boyle was the youngest son of an Irish Protestant blacksmith named Charles, whose own father had immigrated to Upper Canada 20 years before the Potato Famine. After a stint racing thoroughbreds on the U.S. circuits, Charles returned to Canada and settled in Hamilton, where he met Joe's mother, Martha Bain.

Charles continued working with racehorses in Canada as well as breeding his own line of Boyles. In a single decade he sired three sons and a daughter while living in Toronto, and soon after Joe's birth on November 6, 1867, moved the family to a small farm in Newmarket, and then to Woodstock. He became the official timer for the Ontario Jockey Club and in 1883 led his own horse, Rhody Pringle, to the winner's circle of the Queen's Plate, one of Canada's most important annual horse racing events. Charles had a knack for producing winners, and as the trainer for J.E. Seagram, his client's mares won the Queen's Plate for 10 years in a row from 1891 to 1901.

Woodstock was too sleepy a place for restless 17-year-old Joe. His father had once again begun to participate in American racing events and Joe had only his mother and sister to keep him entertained. Longing for a different life, he set out that summer on a roundabout route that took him through the northeastern states before he landed in New York. There, he took up horse work with his father. Joe often stayed with his older brothers in the Kelsey House, a hotel on Lower Broadway, because it gave him the freedom to wander the city away from his father's watchful eye. Often disappearing for hours at a time, Joe would visit the harbour, stare at the clippers, and listen enraptured to the colourful tales of strange ports and dark-eyed women.

On one such excursion, he met the master of the *Wallace*, W.A. Smith, who captained a wooden barque that had been built in Windsor, Nova Scotia only a few years before. Smith saw the glimmer of curiosity in Joe's eye. The young man was intelligent and engaging, strong and eager. He was the perfect candidate for a crewman aboard the *Wallace,* soon to sail for India. Smith might have offered, or Joe may have asked, but what is certain is a few days after meeting Smith, young deckhand-to-be Joe left a note for his brothers and vanished.

"I've gone to sea," he had scribbled. "Don't worry about me. Joe."

His hasty departure on a jaunt to India stretched into three long, arduous years. Joe endured the hardships, though, and revelled in the danger, never once bothering to write home to ease the worry his brothers and parents had for his safety. That self-centred trait was a flaw that marked his life, but perhaps it was just as well the family didn't know about his travails at sea.

Not long after reaching the Indian Ocean, for example, the *Wallace* encountered a massive storm front and nearly sank. While Captain Smith tried to steer his vessel downwind, the *Wallace* swivelled and bucked, diving into the troughs of huge waves, constantly in threat of being pitch poled. The lines screamed under the stress of each blow, the sails groaned, and the crew prayed. When a rogue wave engulfed the ship and snapped the mainmast, the men clawed for a handhold on the slippery deck, realizing the *Wallace*'s hold was filling with seawater. They rigged pumps and strained to keep their tiny vessel from capsizing in a succession of storms that left no time for rest for several days.

But the men seemed to be fighting a losing battle. The pumping had no apparent effect as walls of green water relentlessly swept over the deck in wave after merciless wave. Many bone-weary crewmates simply gave up their place at the pump handles, fatalistically resigning themselves to death. When Joe realized what was happening, a focussed calm came over him. It was a state of assured command that would rise many times as danger threatened his life.

Joe stepped forward in the crisis and urged his crewmates on. The teen took command of his seniors without pause, driving them to pump by using sarcasm and shouting words of encouragement. He said and did whatever it took to keep the men pumping until the storm passed. The men were still at the pumps days later when the crippled *Wallace* finally limped into port.

While in India, young, mop-haired Joe had plenty of opportunity to showcase his other talents. In port, the sailors often tried to entertain each other with songs and jigs on deck and Joe was a favourite performer. He had a natural ear for music, could easily memorize tunes and lyrics, and would improvise with the smallest amount of encouragement. Though Joe had never been formally taught, his baritone voice accompanied any stringed instrument he could find on board. Moreover, when music wasn't wanted, he kept his crewmates entertained with other attractions. Joe organized boxing matches against the crews of other ships, usually placing bets on himself.

He might have remained at sea all his life had it not been for a period of poor business encountered by the *Wallace.* The ship often sat idle for long stretches in out-of-the way ports, waiting for a cargo. Captain Smith was losing money and decided it was time to head for home. Joe, however, said he had more of the world still to see. He signed on as a deckhand on a ship bound for England instead.

The new ship's master managed to run that vessel aground off the coast of Ireland, giving Joe a few short weeks to visit the land of his forefathers before taking a job as first mate on the *Susan,* a small cargo schooner bound for New York. Joe, who'd saved his pay from the *Wallace,* probably used his money to buy a share in the cargo on the *Susan* for his return voyage across the Atlantic.

After arriving in the American port city, Joe made his way through the roughest part of the dock district in a freshly tailored English suit. Even though his pockets were crammed with cash, he had no fear of assault, having survived far worse slums and dangerous surroundings. He found his brother Dave still living at the Kelsey House. The older Boyle was surprised to see his baby brother transformed into such a physically superb specimen. Dave shuffled Joe off to a barber, and telegraphed their parents with the good news of Joe's return. Then he organized a welcome home celebration.

Party guests were mostly other residents at the hotel. Among them was a gay, attractive divorcée Dave had been quietly courting. Mildred Josephine Raynor knew how to enjoy herself. She had no trouble finding time to socialize, even with a two-year-old named "little Bill" to care for. Her introduction to the handsome, well-heeled sailor was welcomed warmly. Joe entertained the party guests with fascinating stories about his voyages, and before the evening ended, invited Mildred to dinner and a show the following night.

Dave, much shyer and more restrained, didn't speak up to remind Mildred she had already agreed to dine with him that evening. It proved to be a lucky mistake for the older brother.

Joe had plenty of cash and was intent on settling down. With some ample helpings of her company, he fell for Mildred hard and fast. Within three days he'd proposed and the couple married. Joe, the wandering sibling, had swept Dave's hopes away even though it's likely Mildred had told him of his brother's affectionate overtures.

With a new wife and child to suddenly care for, Joe needed a job. He sold his cargo interest in the *Susan* and used the money to invest in a feed and freighting business. With his gift of the gab and a ready clientele in his father's horse racing acquaintances, Joe found quick success. His business skills were sharp. Before long, profits were such that he could afford to buy his pretty wife a home on 93rd Street in New York, followed by another in Red Bank, New Jersey. The household came complete with grooms, coachmen, servants, and a nurse for Bill and the couple's first child, Joe Jr. Joe showered gifts on Mildred, a woman with such a penchant for luxury that the family bestowed her with the unkind nickname of "Mink."

After their marriage, instead of retiring to domesticity, Mildred's fun-loving way of life escalated. She was a social climber. Her whirl of society fetes and expensive dinner parties belied a shallow snobbery. The two people were opposites in the extreme. Joe was frugal and pensive, even to the point of being sullen when others rationed his privacy or freedom. Mildred was a spendthrift, flighty, and pretentious.

While Joe tried to be accommodating, the couple clashed often over the course of several years. Mildred gave birth to a number of children who died prematurely. During this time, Joe lost interest in his feed business and turned his attention to a sport that fit his still superb physical condition so well — boxing. By deciding to manage the Hoboken Athletic Club in New Jersey rather than slave over feed orders and freight schedules, he shunted his family a good distance from Mildred's snobbish crowd.

On June 16, 1896, Joe met Frank Slavin, a lumbering Australian boxer known as the "Sydney Cornstalk." The new friendship probably added to the list of reasons why Joe and Mildred eventually separated. The boxer had a long string of tough bouts on his record as he fought his way up the ladder to the World Heavyweight Championship. He had the aged boxing king, John L. Sullivan, in his sights.

The day the two men met, Frank "Paddy" Slavin had faced American boxer Jake Kilrain at the Hoboken Club. After only two minutes of the first round, the fight was called. Kilrain was awarded a technical knockout and the furious Aussie, known for his ability to take punishment, claimed the bout had been called prematurely.

Slavin turned to Joe, who promptly offered to manage this stiff punching Aussie, believing Slavin had a chance of beating Sullivan if a bout could be arranged. Over the next five months, Joe promoted three more fights in New York and Philadelphia and got his boxer on a list of five contenders for a heavyweight title match. When Sullivan picked the least likely contender for the match, Joe was furious. He arranged a London exhibition between Slavin and a talented black fighter named Peter Jackson in London on May 30, 1892. Joe's departure to England with the boxers marked the impending end of his relationship with Mildred.

At a ring surrounded by English nobility, Slavin got the 10-round beating of his life. Embarrassed and disheartened in defeat, Slavin decided to remain in England after the fight, but Joe returned to New York.

By autumn 1896, Joe and Mildred were legally separated. Mildred had given birth to eight children during their nine-year marriage. Before Joe Jr. had arrived, she'd given birth to a premature baby who'd died. After Joe Jr. it was a set of twins who also died soon after birth. Then a daughter, named Macushal, who succumbed to scarlet fever at six months. Macushal's death was followed by the births of two more girls, Flora and Susan.

After making his decision to leave Mildred, Joe acted quickly. Within weeks he liquidated his New York holdings and paid Mildred three-quarters of the proceeds as a settlement. In return for his generosity, Joe wanted custody of Joe Jr., Flora, and Susan, but Mildred refused. To Joe's surprise, Mildred announced she was pregnant again. The conception was a handy means to dispute resolution. Joe took custody of Joe Jr. and Flora. He left Susan and the unborn child, to be called Charlotte, with his wife. They agreed that there would be no further alimony payments and that the divided parts of his household would not communicate with each other again. Then the couple split. Joe's brother Charles took Joe Jr. to his parents' farm in Woodstock. A few months later, Joe took his daughter Flora there too, but it was evident he had no intention of staying there himself.

Joe began talking about the wondrous opportunities waiting for the brave and strong in Alaska. His tales of northern potential may have been spurred by newspaper reports of a Klondike gold strike. Or perhaps he was encouraged by conversations with prominent friends of his father's in Ottawa. Regardless, Joe told his parents he intended to travel north.

First, however, he would give Slavin's quest for a championship another try. Having put his London loss behind him, Slavin had returned from England and was ready to fight again. Shortly after Christmas 1896, Joe kissed the children goodbye and boarded a train.

For months, he and Slavin criss-crossed eastern Canada, earning money from unofficial exhibition matches. Their pay came from the side bets Joe made and from admissions gained with the pass of a hat among whatever group of spectators they could attract. The pickings were slim. It was so bad, in fact, that Joe and Slavin took a job organizing a bowling club for the M. Bartholomew Brewing Company in Rochester, New York just to pay for food.

Had it not been for an offer of a $5000 purse to have Slavin fight a boxer named Johnson in San Francisco on May 21, 1897, Joe might have given up on dreams and returned to his children in Woodstock. But a quiet life working with his father's horses simply wasn't his destiny. Joe asked his father to look after the money he had left from his New York ventures, and then he and Slavin headed west.

Joe was ready to put all his promotional skills to use building a huge audience for the fight with Johnson, but when they arrived in San Francisco on April Fools' Day, 1897, he learned that the fight had been cancelled. The other boxer refused to enter the ring with Slavin.

For several weeks the men were idle. Joe still wanted to get to Alaska and reasoned that the wild frontier town of Juneau, where bare knuckle fighting was still met with enthusiastic support, would be a suitable venue for Slavin's hard-hitting style. To get there, however, they needed a grubstake.

Joe promoted a match between the "Sydney Cornstalk" and another boxer he didn't know named Joe Butler. The pay for the bout would be $1000, win or lose. Though Slavin was far from fighting trim, he convinced Joe to bet the purse on his victory. A win would set them up with all the cash they'd need.

Slavin, old compared to Butler, got the second pummelling of his life. Their grubstake vanished. Joe wired to Woodstock for his "emergency fund" and purchased two steamboat tickets north. Lightweight Frank Raphael, who had been on the same card as Slavin, came along for the ride aboard the SS *City of Pueblo*, bound for Victoria, British Columbia.

The men arrived in staid Victoria on June 17, 1897, two weeks after their departure. The city was in the middle of Queen Victoria's Diamond Jubilee celebrations, so Joe had no difficulty setting up matches in Victoria Gardens between Slavin, a monster of a man named "Jumbo Roberts" from the HMS *Imperieuse*, and a man named Walker from the *Amphion*. Unfortunately, because of the other celebrations underway, few spectators were willing to pay for their entertainment.

Joe promoted the bouts as best he could, gaining a small amount of publicity in the *Victoria Daily Times*. Tickets for the slugfest were advertised at 50 cents and $1, but Victoria's populace was not enthralled with fisticuffs. Only 50 spectators showed up, not even earning the promoter enough to pay for the rental of the arena.

The former sailor must have felt jinxed. The same day they'd arrived in Victoria, the Canadian Gold Commissioner, William Fawcett, had left the city aboard the SS *City of Topeka,* destined for the Klondike. A few days later, the *Victoria Colonist* printed a report about the gold fever in the north, and Joe could plainly see where his future now lay. He let it be known that he was Alaska-bound, intent on setting up matches for Slavin in the Klondike. Since Joe was going north anyway, a Victoria businessman named Captain Moore, in partnership with a Jewish businessman, offered him a chance to lead an expedition that would blaze a more commercially viable route to the Klondike over the White Pass. The businessmen were hoping for a route that could compete with the backbreaking Chilkoot Trail. Joe accepted the job with only a vague notion of what blazing a trail meant.

Before Joe arrived, gold seekers wanting to reach the Klondike had to travel up the Lynn Canal to Dyea, Alaska. From there they faced a hike directly north along the Taiya River to Finnegan's Point, where the Chilkoot Trail began.

Without passage to the ramshackle port of Dyea

readily available, Joe, Slavin, and Raphael headed to the settlement of Juneau because it appeared to be close to the White Pass region on Joe's map.

In Juneau, in need of money for the next leg of their trip and with only $10 between them, Joe promoted a "red hot boxing exhibition" between world-famous pugilist Slavin and a stout contender — Joe himself. With the help of a printer, Joe plastered the community with handbills for his extravaganza. On the afternoon of the fight, he sold 100 tickets at $5 a piece to the entertainment-starved men he found in the town's saloons. However, as the crowds gathered to watch the match, a line of rifle-toting soldiers also entered the hall.

Juneau was under the administration of the United States army, and the commander had strict orders not to condone disorderly behaviour within town limits. A bare-fisted brawl met that definition and he forced a halt to the proceedings.

The spectators answered the commandant's announcement with jeers. Joe realized he was in a stew of trouble. He wouldn't have the money to pay for the hall or the printer if he was forced to give back any of the gate receipts. Knowing he needed to act fast, he took to the makeshift ring and made an announcement of his own.

"I didn't know there was any regulation against boxing in this camp," he shouted to the crowd, "or I wouldn't have sold you tickets. It's clear there can be no exhibition, but I see a piano in that corner, and if you will kindly excuse me a few minutes, Mr. Slavin will give an exhibition of bag punching. After that, it will be up to me and the piano. And I beg to state that if any gentleman desires to have his money back, he can get it."

The spectators seemed willing to accept Joe's alternative to a good, bloody fistfight. Slavin went to work on the bag while Joe dressed. When the Aussie was exhausted, Joe took to the piano and began to play, tell jokes, and sing in his rich baritone voice. To raucous applause he finished a 90-minute performance and then, at the crowd's appreciative urging, went on for 20 minutes more.

At the end of it all, with neither a bloodied nose nor bruised knuckle between them, Joe, Slavin, and Raphael were able to board another boat and head farther north on the Lynn Canal towards Skagway.

Sugarloaf mountains rose on either side of Skagway situated in a narrow glaciated valley at the head of the Taiya Inlet. Translated from its Native Tlingit name "Skaqua," Skagway means "the place where the north wind blows." Even arriving in mid-July, the men learned the area had been well named. They found a collection of tents and miners' goods stacked haphazardly on the beach, and nothing pleasant to recommend the place. Nevertheless, they were happy.

Joe wrote his parents from Skagway and noted that he and Slavin had just 50 cents when they'd arrived, which they'd spent on a shared cup of coffee.

Their White Pass destination was about 300 metres lower than the Chilkoot Pass. Rumours were floating around Skagway that surveyors had found a route to Lake Bennett over the White Pass, though this was a longer trek to the Klondike gateway. Joe, Slavin, and Raphael waited in Skagway for the supplies that Joe's Victoria backers had sent. When the supplies arrived, with the promise of an easier trek, the trio was able to easily gather a group of 14 volunteers with 25 packhorses willing to take on the challenge of the new route. They left Skagway around July 20, 1897.

The trail to the White Pass had a deceptive beginning, winding northeast from Skagway like a wagon road etched between tall pine trees. But just a few kilometres along the wagon road it constricted into a half-metre wide path that twisted along the Skagway River for 72 kilometres. The trail snaked over slippery slate precipices, along the edges of 150-metre drops, and across torrents of running mud that threatened to sweep the unwary hikers down the mountainside. Amid moving clouds of flies and mosquitoes the men had to navigate sinkholes that were so large they could swallow horses. They had to scramble over boulders three metres high with heavy packs containing a year's worth of supplies on their backs.

The trail was barely passable. The Sunday walk to the summit of the pass took the group three long, gruelling days. They were lucky to have gone when they did. By September (and until the ground froze and snow fell) it would become an impossible route.

At the top of the summit, Joe could make out Lake Bennett on the horizon. The surveyed part of trail they'd been following ended at White Pass and six of the men, said to have "icicle feet," decided to turn back. Joe took command.

He told the party he would carry on alone to Lake Bennett and mark the best route he could find. Slavin, in charge of the party, would follow his markings after they had widened the trail from Skagway to the summit. With only eight men to do the work, Slavin quickly returned to Skagway and recruited 20 more men now willing to chance the trek because a route to the summit of White Pass had indeed been found.

Joe slogged through the bush to Lake Bennett. By early August, Slavin's party had succeeded in widening the path from Skagway to the White Pass, and following Joe's trail of cairns, they reached the lake as well. The route Joe had blazed later became the same one the narrow-gauge Whitehorse and Yukon Railway would use.

Several hundred gold seekers' tents dotted the rocky shores of Lake Bennett when Joe Boyle's party finally arrived. Even though the gold strike was now almost a year old, the eager prospectors at the lake were hard at work cutting logs into planks to build boats for the 550-kilometre boat journey to Dawson, the centre of the gold rush. Many more would soon follow them.

At 6 a.m. the day before Joe took off his boots and splashed in Lake Bennett's icy waters, the steamship *Portland* had arrived at Schwabacher's Dock in Seattle to the rousing cheers of 5000 people eager to get the latest information about the gold strike. Thousands were ready to fight for a berth on the next boat heading north. By the following spring, 30,000 men and women would be camped along the shores of Lindeman, Bennett, and Tagish lakes.

North West Mounted Police (NWMP) officers guided the men at Lake Bennett in the rough art of boat construction. "Build them strong," they advised. "Don't end up in a floating coffin." The job of cutting planks took at least two men. One stood on scaffolding above a log and the other below it, and together they guided a two-metre whipsaw along a chalk line. The effort to cut straight boards caused so many partnership failures that Lake Bennett's shore was given the moniker of "Split-Up City."

Thanks to Joe's advance planning, no log cutting had to be done before his group continued their journey down river. Among the tons of supplies they had hauled were the pieces for an eight-metre collapsible boat. The boat proved quite suited to the treacherous currents of Miles Canyon, where the Yukon River drives through a narrow, man-killing gorge. It also proved a stable floating taxi in the Squaw and the Whitehorse Rapids. Very much alive and barely wet, Joe's group reached the calm waters of Lake Laberge without incident, and from there it was just a lazy ride down the Yukon River to Dawson.

Chapter 2
Golden Fantasies

The Klondike district was a 2000-square-kilometre area defined by the Indian River in the south, the Klondike River in the north, and the Yukon in the west. Creeks that fed into the river system — the Bonanza, Quigley, Bear, and Hunker — marked the spots where gold had been discovered.

When Joe, Slavin, and Raphael reached Dawson, they found a desolate looking place. Dawson sat on a wide, flat stretch of marshy ground with the high, avalanche-scarred ridge of the Midnight Dome looming on the horizon to the north. Larger trees lined the banks of the swift-flowing Yukon River. The shore was pocked by tents of all shapes and sizes, and by the hundreds of roughly made watercraft that had floated from Lake Bennett.

With only $22 between them, there was a sense of urgency for Joe and Slavin to find either gold of their own or jobs. There was no shortage of work for labourers with a pick and a shovel. Joe set out immediately to find a job on one of the side creeks. He soon got work at No. 13 Eldorado for the standard pay rate of $15 per day. The pay was welcome, as food in Dawson was precious and expensive. Flour sold for $8 a sack and eggs for $4 a dozen.

Joe worked constantly, by necessity. Winter was not far off and he wanted to learn as much as he could, as quickly as he could, about the secrets of placer mining. (Unlike hard rock mining, in which deep shafts are dug into the ground, placer mining involves sifting through surface gravel, using water and gravity in sluices and shaker boxes, to recover gold.) It didn't take him long to come to the conclusion that a single man's labour was the wrong way to get at the gold locked in the Klondike permafrost. Placer mining by hand recovered only 25 percent of the gold, leaving 75 percent still in the river and creek bottoms. The permafrost was practically unassailable with a pick, so hydraulic mining seemed the most sensible way to approach the moiling. Other miners had ignored the wide timbered valleys alongside the river that were the ideal spots for mining with machinery.

In an 1899 story published by the *Dawson Daily News,* Joe was reported to have "argued that hydraulic mining was the only method and set to work to get blocks of ground."

It was a huge task. Staking a single claim in the area was next to impossible without an investment in an already operating enterprise. But somehow, Joe and Slavin managed to acquire ownership in four claims and shared a tiny log cabin on the hillside behind Dawson.

The Canadian government reacted slowly to the buzz of the Klondike but when the politicians finally did react, they caused an administrative nightmare. The cabinet decided to reduce creek claims to 33-metre frontages, imposed a 20 percent royalty on any claim producing more than $500 a day, and reserved every alternate claim for the Crown. When the miners rebelled, the cabinet reduced the royalty to 10 percent, let creek frontage climb to 75 metres, and allowed miners to make claims in 10-block sections. Every alternate section, rather than every alternate claim, would be reserved for the Crown.

When Order-in-Council PC 125 was made to allow

for dredging operations, Joe and Slavin decided they needed to head to Ottawa. A dredging operation would take capital they didn't have, and special protections for dredging rights could only be obtained through a face-to-face meeting with the minister of the interior, Sir Clifford Sifton.

Joe and Slavin had made many friends among the restless souls and entrepreneurs who'd flocked to Dawson. Of particular note was the friendship Joe had developed with William C. Gates. Short, flamboyant "Swiftwater Gates" was an American who, along with five others, had bought a 30-metre piece of No. 13 Eldorado. Their "lay," a part-claim in Klondike parlance, had been worked with seven shafts. Only one proved to contain gold, but it had a lot.

Using some of his earnings from No. 13 Eldorado, Gates had partnered with Jack Smith to run a saloon called the Monte Carlo. The saloon was part bar, part brothel, and part casino, and it made more money for Gates than the claim ever could.

In late August 1897, Gates and Joe left on an upriver trek to Whitehorse. Gates went on the trip to find a fresh stock of California women for the 1898 season at the Monte Carlo. Joe was headed east. Using the collapsible boat that had carried Joe from Lake Bennett, the duo enjoyed easy going for a short time as they poled their way towards Whitehorse. By September 24, however, the weather shifted dramatically. Winter was approaching with a vengeance. Pack ice quickly formed on the waterway and soon damaged the boat so badly that the men were forced to abandon it and make their way to the still-distant Carmack's Post on foot.

The 400 kilometres from Dawson to Carmack's Post was a harrowing slog. On one occasion, Gates fell through the river ice and was rescued in the nick of time by Joe. When the duo finally made it to the tiny settlement, they found a group of stranded men. Among them were four men who were carrying the U.S. mail, and others heading to Dawson including Jack London, the writer.

The weather was miserable and the men waited a full month for it to break before Joe and Gates decided it was time to move on October 29. Several of the stranded agreed that if they travelled together, pooling their meagre resources, they stood a better chance of reaching the next settlement shelter at Haines Mission alive. In summer, the 160-kilometre journey was possible in just four days, but with blizzards blasting the group and –30°C temperatures, it took the eight-man party 25 days. Snow was waist deep or higher, and not long after the group began, the men had to shoot the pack horses because they couldn't move in the deep snow. Many

Joe (on the left) with Swiftwater Bill Gates in 1897. Joe was 29 years old at the time of the epic journey to Whitehorse.

times, members of the exhausted party were prepared to lay down in the freezing Yukon tomb and die, but Joe refused to allow them to stop. Like the time he drove his shipmates at the pumps in mighty ocean gales, Joe encouraged, exhorted, and even cursed the men into moving forward.

On November 23, 1897, they reached Haines Mission at the mouth of the Chilkat River and almost immediately got passage on the SS *City of Seattle*. The men were carrying $12,000 in Klondike gold. When they finally arrived in Seattle, Gates took a bath in a tub of champagne to celebrate, and the grateful group hosted a dinner for their saviour, Joe. They presented him with an engraved gold watch to signify their appreciation for his courage and leadership.

"Every man of the party," the *Dawson Daily News* reported a year later, "except Joe himself, declares till this day that but for his able management not a man would have reached the coast alive."

Having delivered the delayed U.S. mail in Seattle, Joe took a train to eastern Canada, intent on concluding his business there. He spent a short time in Woodstock visiting his children and recuperating before moving on again to Ottawa and Montreal. Shortly after New Year's of 1898, Slavin joined his partner.

In a well-organized plan, Slavin had made an application to lease a large 13-kilometre tract of river frontage and filed it with the Gold Commissioner in Dawson on December 1, 1897. In the meantime, Joe had begun searching for a financial partner in their scheme. The process of luring new capital was difficult. Besides the potential claim, Joe had little but his own character and ideas to add to any partnership. The mining plan he proposed, however practical, still held risk.

Parliament convened on February 3, 1898. Two days later, Joe met with Clifford Sifton and discussed his claim application to do hydraulic mining (from the Upper Ferry on the Klondike near the mouth of Bonanza Creek, upstream about 15 kilometres to Hunker Creek). Sifton was probably eager to meet with Joe and learn more about Dawson. He had tried to reach the Klondike with a group of civil servants the previous October, but the same storms that had nearly killed Joe had forced Sifton to turn back at Skagway. When Joe described the trials of will and the challenges of privation he'd faced travelling from Dawson to Whitehorse, Sifton was probably all ears. Joe must have thought he had gained a friend "at court."

Joe settled in at the Russell Hotel to await ministerial approval of the application, expecting it within days. But the wait stretched into weeks and then months. Joe sent Slavin back to Dawson to work the claims they had staked the previous autumn. Earlier, Joe had made a verbal deal with the Canadian Yukon Company in Montreal for his financing, based on getting Sifton's approval. When this approval failed to arrive, the financing collapsed.

Joe promptly wrote to Sifton, claiming the delays had cost him an investor and a full season of work. He demanded immediate approval of the claim application.

Sifton reacted by requesting further negotiations, but the claim was soon approved in principle. The deal cost Joe 10 percent in royalties on mine output in excess of $5000, but he managed to get a tax concession on the first $20,000 per year because he had to buy, ship, and operate the machinery for the claim. It appears that the Ottawa minions were delaying because they didn't give Joe much credit, thinking he was over-reaching himself with his grandiose plan.

In mid-June, Joe headed back to the Yukon with verbal assurance that the claim would be approved. He arrived on July 7, 1898, to find that Slavin had been unable to protect their new concession. Another miner, named Stewart, had encroached on the property for a 6.5-kilometre stretch of river north of Bonanza Creek, protecting his conquest with gun-toting miners and lumberjacks. Stewart, it seems, had been cutting the slow-growing Yukon timber along the shore with a crew of about 50 men.

Joe had a letter from Sifton that supposedly froze action in the case of a timber dispute until a ruling could be received from Ottawa. It made no difference to Stewart. Neither did the No Trespassing signs Joe posted. Finally, to protect his and Slavin's interests, Joe hired a gang of gunmen of his own and posted them on the claim. Then he headed back to Ottawa.

The Stewart incident proved to Joe that he needed much more protection on the concession if he was to make money. Using a battery of lawyers, he prompted the cabinet to agree to a fresh policy granting him a timber licence on his claim.

The cabinet's ruling in Joe's favour was a divisive one to the miners in Dawson, who were impatiently waiting for a supply of timber for everything from campfires to sluice boxes and roads. Joe didn't worry about currying any favour. By early 1899, he and Slavin had built a sawmill on the claim, and that autumn, Joe organized a group of teamsters to lay a slab road in Dawson. Then he went to work building a fortune off his sawmill's product.

A cord of wood that had been selling for $18 the previous December was advertised the following month at $48, a cost that was 250 percent inflated. Joe was applying the same business acumen that he'd shown building his New York freight business, but while he was shrewd and hard working, his partner Paddy Slavin was the opposite. Slavin began devoting more of his time to boxing and the easy money it brought him. Perhaps a little punch-drunk, and willing to imbibe even in the presence of Joe, who neither smoked nor drank alcohol, it wasn't long before Slavin was demoted from partner to employee. Joe paid Slavin $20,000 for his interest in 17 jointly held claims.

Joe rapidly began an almost avaricious drive to accumulate wealth. As early as September 1898, he had bought several pieces of real estate in Dawson, had a six-metre wharf, a 30-metre warehouse, a lumber dock, half an interest in another hydraulic grant from Canyon to Caulder on Quartz Creek, and 16 placer claims in his name. However, by June 9, 1899, Joe still hadn't formally received his hydraulic concession.

He wrote to Sifton to complain again, and to ask for the renewal of his lucrative timber licences as well. Joe had no idea that Sifton was in negotiations with another man of their mutual acquaintance named Treadgold, who was trying to organize a monopoly on concessions in the Klondike and thereby steal the water rights to foil Joe's plans for hydraulic mining.

Joe knew that the timber was as important as the hydraulic concession. He now had two sawmills, and they had cut more than a 300,000 metres of logs in 1899. In a short period of a year, Joe had become a very wealthy man from his "woodlot." He'd also formed another plan for concession exploitation with Swiftwater Bill Gates. Both men had properties along Quartz River, and in the late fall of 1899, they moved heavy hydraulic equipment to the mouth of the river, intending to haul it to their mining site on the winter ice.

Joe's effort at wealth building and acquisition was amazing. That autumn, he was lauded for it by his peers in a special mining edition of the *Dawson Daily News*. "Although Mr. Boyle has worked hard and incessantly, his work has had no ill effects for there is no finer specimen of physical manhood in the world today — his magnificent physique, great strength and happy, sympathetic nature, coupled with a total abstinence from the use of liquor and tobacco, make him an ideal character for this rigorous climate."

In December 1899, Joe decided he needed a holiday, or perhaps had new plans in mind, and left Dawson on a trip to Woodstock and then Ottawa. Following a visit with the children, he went to the capital and then took passage to London, England. Even with plenty of collateral, he was unable to attract investor interest in his Klondike claims. However, he did have the confidential knowledge that he would soon have a hydraulics lease that was good for a 20-year period (claim no. 18 was later approved by cabinet on November 5, 1900). He returned to Dawson and got back to his empire building.

While Joe was away from the North, business hadn't been the only thing on his mind. On July 19, 1899, a new Mrs. Boyle arrived "from the outside." Her origins were uncertain and mysterious, as was her departure from his life only a few years later. On July 11, 1903, Mrs. Boyle, a wife by reputation only, left Dawson and boarded the *Selkirk,* one of the 10 steamers that were being operated then by the White Pass and Yukon Route Company. She stated her plan was to visit her mother in California. She never came back.

A new moral respectability had gripped the boomtown of Dawson after the frenzied rush of activity a few years earlier. The red light district of "Lousetown" had been the first to go. By 1903, gambling was outlawed in Dawson, the music halls were shut down, and known prostitutes were forced out. Mrs. Boyle's departure seemed oddly coincidental with the prim attitudes that were blossoming in the permafrost "muck."

Aside from hunting, there was little else in Dawson to distract Joe from work. He hired his brother Charlie to manage part of his business affairs while he entertained in small, private ways. A Swede he'd met named Edward Bredenberg, for example, became a close confidant. Teddy Bredenberg had arrived in the Yukon in 1898, and he shared many interests with Joe. He too had stolen away to sea, but at the age of 14.

Joe's financial position in Dawson was envied nearly to the point of being a personal burden to the otherwise very generous man. Other miners stood at the ready, waiting eagerly to jump his claim and steal his timber if Joe ever made an operating mistake within the terms of his lease deal. His property was under the constant threat of thieves, and the way Joe squeezed profits from his operations left many with bad attitudes towards him. He may have felt it was time to withdraw.

In June 1904, he was finally able to work a deal on his claims with Sigmund Rothschild of the Detroit-Yukon Mining Company. On June 18, Elmer Bremer of Detroit-Yukon announced his company was going to put a steam shovel at the mouth of Bear Creek. Bremer moved into the original log cabin that Joe and Slavin had built, and set up shop for the company.

Joe expected to see a new era of mechanized mining in the Yukon, with himself at the top of a wealthy pyramid. But his expectations were soon proven wrong.

At 38 years old, Joe appeared to have lost his desire for mining enterprise. If he had to stay in Dawson and run a business, he decided to do it with some active diversions. One of these diversions was hockey.

The Stanley Cup, which had been donated by Lord Stanley of Preston in 1893, represented a new goal for Joe. The Dawson Athletic Club had donated level land where, on November 24, 1899, the idle soldiers of the Yukon Field Force had flooded an ice rink. Hockey soon became popular among the miners during their long months of winter boredom. By the 1901–1902 season, Dawson had organized league competitions on the ice, and the club announced it would build a modern club-house with a covered arena.

Hockey turned into an obsession in the Yukon. Skilled players who'd made a name in the east were gradually found playing on one or other of the northern league teams. Joe hired some ringers himself, finding them daytime work in his enterprise. In other cases, civil servants with hockey skills found themselves inexplicably transferred to the North. The spectators and players were soon boasting that some of the best hockey in Canada was being played before the $1 reserved seating in Dawson.

Then someone raised a vagrant thought. Let's take our best team on the road. In fact, our team is so good, let's challenge for that piece of tin they call the Cup. Sometime in July, that challenge was made official, and Joe was named as the Klondike Hockey Club's representative to arrange the eastern dates for their team's tour.

The Klondike team would not be allowed to play exhibition games if they wanted to compete for the Cup. Joe re-named the team the Yukon Nuggets and announced that after the best-two-of-three Cup series, the Nuggets would go on a nation-wide hockey tour. The team had to walk out of Dawson to Whitehorse that winter because of a lack of snow. Some even took to the trail on bicycles. And though they all reached Whitehorse on schedule, a blizzard caused them to miss catching the boat they had planned on taking to the south.

On a schedule that would have had the team arriving in Ottawa four days before the start of play, the Nuggets finally departed Skagway on a Seattle-bound vessel three days late. They were five days behind schedule when, after a horrendously rough sea voyage, they reached Vancouver and boarded the Canadian Pacific Railway trans-continental. Pleas by the team to have the match delayed a few days so they could recuperate from their miserable ordeal of a trip were rejected, and the series opener was slated to begin on schedule.

Only the *Ottawa Citizen* gave the team credit for their great effort. "The spectacle of a team travelling 4000 miles and at an expense neighbouring around $6000 … [is] something calculated to overawe anyone not aware of the popularity of Canada's great winter game."

On the day before the game, the Nuggets had one — and only one — chance to practice for the series. Due to their extended travel time, they hadn't been on the ice in a month. The Ottawa team, however, was a finely tuned machine.

More than 2500 spectators crammed Dey's Arena for the Friday, January 13th showdown. The Nuggets lost the first game 9–2. Joe claimed Ottawa made four offside goals. One of the Yukon players received a 15-minute penalty for breaking his stick over the head of an Ottawa player. The game was rough to say the least. But the second game was even rougher on the Nuggets. Ottawa won 23–2.

After the tour that followed, Joe sent his boys home with a bonus for their efforts but decided to stay in the East himself. It was the beginning of a four-year hiatus from the North. He didn't return to the Yukon until 1909.

Financial pressure had been building on Joe for some time. Criticism about his concession had grown to the point that he considered selling out.

In the spring of 1904, Joe re-evaluated an offer from the Detroit Mining Company, and that summer Sigmund Rothschild officially offered him an astounding $750,000 for the concession. To put it into context, at the time of the deal, Eaton's was selling leather boots for $6. A train trip from Toronto to Atlantic City went for the huge sum of $11, and the finest of suits could be had for only $25.

The Detroit Mining Company said it was going to dredge for gold, but two months later the deal was withdrawn. Instead, Rothschild proposed a joint stock company. Rather than the original price, Detroit Mining would invest $500,000 in cash and issue 30,000 shares of which Joe would own a third. He would receive the other $250,000 from royalties on gross gold production by a new company called the Canadian Klondyke Mining Company Limited (CKMC). Joe's 10,000 shares were to be paid off over a three-year period, the schedule for which Joe would not be able to control as a minority shareholder.

It was a bad deal, but Joe accepted and went to Woodstock to spend time with Joe Jr. and Flora. He travelled to London, New York, and Detroit, spending much of his time sequestered in lawyers' offices. And there were other complications in his life.

Millie, who had been separated from Joe for eight years but never divorced, suddenly appeared in Woodstock with Charlotte and Susan. Despite their separation agreement, she wanted more money. When Joe flatly refused her, Millie went to the Ottawa newspapers and told them she intended to file for divorce. She named as corespondent an actress called Jessie Wyatt whom Joe had met in 1897–98.

"Mr. Boyle," the press said, "was greatly impressed with Miss Wyatt's attainments and induced her to go to Dawson."

Millie seemed to have the goods on Joe. He offered her a substantial annual payment in settlement for a divorce, but "Mink" thought she could squeeze for more. She was wrong. She pursued the divorce in Chicago in 1907 and was awarded $50 a week in alimony.

Joe then turned a watchful eye on Detroit Mining. Rothschild had brought four partners with him into the syndicate to buy Joe's concession. Each was to have placed $100,000 in cash into the deal to pay for development of the property. When Joe learned that the $500,000 had been written off by selling the old company machinery along with two worthless claims it held near the Joe property, he knew he was in financial trouble.

But if he was going to get swindled, he was ready to put up a bloody fight. To avoid publicity, he hired a Woodstock lawyer named Wallace Nesbitt. During months of quiet preparation for his court assault against the syndicate, Joe ignored the company and his property. Rothschild had been expansive in publicizing his plans. They had one dredge and had ordered another. On July 25, 1906, the company announced it had recorded a day's tally of $5000 in gold. Joe waited patiently for the moment when he could launch his lawsuit and reclaim what rightfully belonged to him.

It finally happened early in 1907, when Rothschild

sold 10,000 shares of CKMC to the Guggenheims for $110,000. Joe claimed that with this sale of shares, he had become the largest company shareholder. His action was to be heard in October in Sandwich, Ontario.

The court ruled that the original agreement did not entail the purchase of any equipment, and that the syndicate partners were therefore required to pay court costs and deposit the $500,000 agreed upon into the company treasury. The Detroit syndicate countered with another lawsuit in the United States. They attempted to restrain Joe from any further involvement in the company, and claimed that a $190,000 deposit made to the treasury was enough when $310,000 in offsetting bills was tallied.

When the syndicate members failed to pay court costs for Joe's initial lawsuit, the CKMC was placed into receivership and Joe was appointed the receiver. He had to obtain a $300,000 bond to meet his obligations as the receiver, and this left the syndicate members one more chance to challenge him. Joe was required to put up another $150,000, and on May 22, the Ontario Divisional Court revoked his appointment. Joe tried to appeal and it took a year for his case to be heard. The judges ruled that there were "no substantial grounds" to remove management from the syndicate members.

Proving he was not to be intimidated by the Detroit

moneymen, Joe immediately filed two more suits: one against CKMC, and one against the company directors. The added suits sent the syndicate members running. Joe was able to purchase their 20,000 shares for $20 each, paid without interest in three yearly instalments.

When Joe returned to the Klondike, he was accompanied by a new wife. He'd married Elma Louise Humphries in Detroit during the spring of 1909. Elma was a quiet, gentle woman who had worked as a manicurist in a hotel where Joe had stayed while in Detroit. She might have been his practical means of avoiding the incessant approaches of gold diggers trying to make the rich "King of the Klondike" their catch. Joe had also brought his daughter Flora back with him to his house on Bear Creek.

Joe's brother Charles had been living in the home and was managing Joe's business affairs. Charles was now married, so Joe solved the space crisis by doubling the size of the house.

Upon his return to the Klondike, Joe found some aspects of his business in disarray. Squatters had been allowed to settle on parts of his land. With dredging operations scheduled to begin, Joe needed to displace them. Rather than force them away without concern for their welfare, he dealt with the squatters in a fair manner, discussing his problem and theirs, and then paying each to help them move. Such acts, and his constant support of charitable activities in Dawson, perhaps changed the prevailing negative attitude towards him in that northern city.

"...Only those associated with him closely will appreciate his broadmindedness, his capacity for long, laborious and efficient effort, drawing heavily on his marvellously rugged physique without apparent exhaustion. He always has a foundation of clear and logical thinking, and his mind works rapidly in the grasp of detail and general plans. He never fails in the keen appreciation of the human side of things and he is ever an inspiration to the men under his direction." *Dawson Daily News*

Chapter 3
Bring on the Hun

On August 4, 1914, when the radio reported that Great Britain had declared war on Imperial Germany, Joe stood with the rest of the Dawson population in the Amateur Athletic Association theatre and sang "God Save the King."

He knew, regretfully, that the world had changed with the British cabinet's call to arms, and he felt frustration rising within. He was 46 years old; too old to bear personal witness or offer service in the military.

Since he couldn't be a soldier himself, he resolved to live vicariously though the heroism he knew would be performed by the younger men in Dawson. Joe approached Yukon member of parliament Dr. Alfred Thompson, who was hurriedly packing for a trip to Ottawa, and asked a favour. He wanted the MP to meet with Sam Hughes, the minister in militia and defence, and tell him that Joe was willing to raise, pay, and outfit a special 50-man Yukon corps for overseas service. He wanted the government to name the corps after a controversial new weapon called a "machine gun." The Yukon men were to join units supplied by Eaton and Borden as part of two detachments in the First Canadian Machine Gun Corps.

Hughes accepted Joe's offer on September 2, along with similar offers from a half-dozen other private citizens across Canada. Within four days, recruiting officers were signing men for Joe's Dawson brigade. Joe arranged for the men to be taught the basics of army drill by the Royal North West Mounted Police. The new recruits also received lessons on how to shoot by experts in the local rifle association.

Yukon men, eager to fight for their king, weren't hard to find. With a Husky sled dog named Jack as their mascot, Joe saw the brigade off from the Dawson dock on October 10, 1914.

In the months that followed, Joe worked diligently at maintaining production by the Canadian Klondyke

Mining Company, which had lost its most experienced men to the war. He also maintained contact with Sam Hughes to track the progress of his brigade.

The men had been shipped to military camp in Vancouver by October 27 as part of the 29th Battalion of the Canadian Expeditionary Force, and they remained in Vancouver for some time. It wasn't until February 18, 1915, that Joe's detachment got official authorization. When April arrived and the men were still at Hastings Park, several were prepared to quit what they saw as a charade.

On behalf of his grumbling unit, Joe wrote directly to the minister, imploring him to have the Yukon detachment sent overseas, even if it meant they had to go without horses. Hughes saw the order carried out. The men departed Canada on June 11, 1915, aboard the *Megantic*, and when they arrived in England eight days later, they were absorbed into the Eaton Motor Machine Gun Brigade as the "Boyle Battery." On June 19, Joe wrote to thank the minister and to ask why he had still not been billed for the unit's machine guns. He received no explanation. In early July, the unit was attached to the Canadian Division and moved to France.

The redeployment didn't satisfy Joe much. He was flushed with anti-German fervour, even posting a notice to warn his employees that anyone espousing pro-German views, or anyone failing to report others with those views, would be fired. He fumed upon learning that George Black, the gold commissioner and not a young man by any means, had gone to Ottawa, and with political pull had managed to raise and lead a 200-man Yukon force. Meanwhile, Joe was forced to sit at home and read the newspaper dispatches. Worse, his battery wasn't seeing action at all.

Perhaps he was looking for a reason to get closer to his men, because on July 27, 1916, Joe left Dawson and headed for London. Officially his goal was to negotiate a deal with South African Goldfields Company over a vast gold mining venture in Russia. He had also agreed to consult on the proposed construction of a five-metre bucket-type dredge, like the ones he was using at Bear Creek, for the Lenisky Company of London, who were considering its use on the Lena River in Siberia.

Joe arrived in London in August, around the same time as Sir Sam Hughes. Hughes had gone to England to finalize plans for the organization of Canada's Expeditionary Force in Britain. The Yukoner must have impressed on the strong-willed, flamboyant minister that it was only appropriate a financial supporter be given some kind of recognition. On September 13, 1916, by ministerial directive, Joe was made Honorary Lieutenant-Colonel in charge of the Yukon Machine Gun Battery.

Before year's end, Joe had purchased several uniforms to match his courtesy title. He replaced the general service badges with badges made from Boyle gold, and had gold-embroidered flashes sewn at the sleeve tops to carry the name "Yukon." Joe did his best to seek a role with the Canadian Expeditionary Force, but was unsuccessful. He spent the remainder of the fall dealing long distance with problems in Dawson, visiting relatives, and meeting with friends. Among these friends was Herbert Hoover, a mining engineer who had known Joe for some time. Hoover was part of Granville Mining, a company that had loaned Joe millions to build his dredges.

At the time, Joe was in the midst of litigation with Granville Mining over those loans. During the nine months he spent in Britain, he stayed at the Savoy Hotel, but more often found himself cooling his heels in the London law courts.

When the United States joined the war on April 6, 1917, Joe found an opportunity perfectly suited to his skills as a project organizer.

The ad hoc American Committee of Engineers (ACE) had been formed to provide technical advice on special services to the Allies in Europe. The membership had talents ranging from pure science to counter-intelligence. It boasted 59 active and 11 consulting members including Joe's friend Herbert Hoover. Joe also had a favourable relationship with C.W. Purington, the Committee's honorary chairperson, stemming from the consultation Joe had provided to Lena Goldfields Limited. At the time, Europeans had invested as much in Russia as they had in the United States — about $4 billion — and Joe's consultation was recognized as valuable and prestigious.

The ACE was considering 16 projects. One was to ensure the smooth operation of the Russian railways immediately behind the Russian front lines. The ACE was put at the disposal of the French Commission Internationale de Ravitaillement (CIR) for the project, and Joe promptly asked Purington for an assignment. He was put in charge of the ACE mission to Russia to develop the project.

Joe had an excellent set of guidelines to follow. Sir George Bury, a CPR vice-president, had been in Petrograd (now St. Petersburg) at the time of the Russian spring revolution and had written a comprehensive report about what was wrong with the Russian transportation system. Things weren't as clear-cut on the home front, however.

Joe Jr., now a mining engineer, had been placed in charge of the Bear Creek operation without power-of-attorney. He was facing strikes by the workers for back-due wages, equipment problems, and the pending Granville litigation. He wrote his father pleading for instructions, but none were given for seven weeks. Joe Jr. must have been spitting spikes about having been left responsible without legal authority.

The Granville court case was slated for June 20, but Boyle left for Petrograd on June 17 with a secretary and a translator. He travelled via Norway and Sweden and arrived in the city on June 25. Joe's job would be to untangle the Russian military railway lines so supplies could flow unhampered to troops. He was cautioned not to impede a similar effort for the civilian system being undertaken by John F. Stevens, the man who had built the Panama Canal.

Prior to World War I, the German government had worried about being attacked by either France in the west or Russia in the east. In 1879, Germany and Austria-Hungary had formed the Dual Alliance, which became the Triple Alliance in 1882, when it was expanded to include Italy. The three countries had agreed to support each other if attacked by either France or Russia. The Triple Alliance became known as the Central Powers when war broke out. In 1907, Britain, France, and Russia formed their own alliance, which was known as the Triple Entente and then as the Allied Powers with the start of the war.

With the outbreak of hostilities, the advance of the Central Powers into Russia dealt the country a heavy blow. The eventual cost to Russia would be two million soldiers killed, wounded, or captured. When autocratic Tsar Nicholas II abdicated his crown, Russia was facing the turmoil of European war. A provisional government was running Russia, but the Bolshevik party (the revolutionary party of workers) was harassing this government. Russia was in the midst of a revolutionary social reconstruction, and without a steady movement of food supplies to the major cities the nation was starving. Joe appeared between the first and second act in the revolutionary drama.

Wandering through Petrograd, swaggering in his new uniform, complete with a polished ceremonial sword hanging from his hip and gold decorations glinting in the sun, Joe was a sight none of the Russian generals expected. The Russian army officials knew that many of their defeats could be traced directly to the railway's inability to feed and re-arm their front-line troops. How in heaven was this comic version of an officer in a tailored uniform going to make any difference?

Joe's satchel was filled with letters of introduction to various leaders in the provisional government, but his first order of business was to meet with Sir George Buchanan, the British ambassador. Appearing in full regimental garb, Joe paid his respects and calmly told the diplomat he'd come to fix things. This brash declaration by the inexperienced amateur sent waves of panic rippling though the military staff. That included General Frederick C. Poole, the British officer who would soon assume command of the British and Canadian forces in northern Russia.

The ACE hadn't bothered to tell the British military in London what was going on. A hasty cable whipped across the Atlantic from Whitehall to Ottawa. "Can you tell me confidentially whether [Boyle] represents the Canadian government and under whose authority he is acting and what is the real object of his mission?" Ottawa had no idea.

Unaware of any confusion he'd created, Joe charged on and held five meetings with Russian officials over a four-day span. He met General A.A. Manikovski, the Russian assistant commissioner of war, several other generals, and then N.V. Nekrasov, the minister of ways and communications. Joe had hoped to meet Russian war minister Alexander Kerensky as well, but Kerensky was at the front.

The Russians must have been impressed by Joe's confidence and forcefulness. Manikovski in particular seemed to get along well with the Yukon mining man because he immediately suggested Joe travel to Mogilev (now Mahilyow in Belarus), a small provincial town on the Dnieper River southwest of the Russian army head-quarters in Stavka, to begin his investigations.

Joe said he would go, but he gave the assistant commissioner a warning. In his report to the ACE he said: "I told him that there should be but one head man and that any place I went this would be the case."

Joe set off for Mogilev in a sturdy staff car on the afternoon of July 2 and completed the 480-kilometre journey through war-torn countryside by 3 p.m. the following day. He described Mogilev as a "mean and dirty little place populated mostly by Jewes [sic] and Catholics who were forever at loggerheads," and main-tained that the railway was little better than a snarl.

The fact that Joe, with all his bluster, was able to gain audience with the most powerful men in the Russian army headquarters continued to ruffle feathers among the British diplomats. There was another flurry of inquiries. Uppermost in their minds was the possibil-ity that Joe had used the letters of introduction he'd been given by the ACE improperly. The Russians were asking questions of the British about Joe. Who was this man? What was he doing in Russia? What had the British asked of him and therefore them? The British, in a fog of embarrassed ignorance, were unable to provide any more answers than the Canadians. In desperation, they again notified Ottawa of their concern and soon the Directorate of Military Intelligence (DMI) at the War Office became involved. A tracer was immediately put out to find this renegade "civilian" and rein him in.

On July 8, Joe finally met with the commander-in-chief of the Russian armies, General A. Busiloff, to present his letters of introduction and credentials. He'd been in Russia for 12 days and had already made a series of recommendations to the ACE that would see a complete revamping of the way the Russians handled the movement and control of their trains behind the front. Tired but exhilarated after his meeting with Busiloff, Joe boarded a train and headed southwest to Tarnopol (now Ternopil in Ukraine) and to the sound of gunfire.

The Russians had mounted an offensive that had made spectacular progress for a time against the Austro-German forces, but again, the failure to re-supply the troops had brought the progress to a sudden stop. From Tarnopol, Joe engaged himself in forays to meet the various officers in charge along the front lines. He found them all to be apathetic, uninspired, shoddy leaders with no desire to command. Shortages were apparent everywhere. The average daily progress of a locomotive pulling supply cars to the needy troops was a scant 100 kilometres. Saddened and desperate to help, he shot letters and reports to anyone who would listen, asking for equipment and men to relieve the situation. But the matters were too large and the wait for help too long.

Under a rain of falling artillery shells, Joe was forced to retreat from the front with thousands of men. They pulled back to Tarnopol, where he found the city in disarray. Russian headquarters staff had decamped before the retreat, leaving no one in charge of the troops.

Joe later reported that he took action himself. The German army was advancing on the city and could have enjoyed an easy victory over the unprepared Russians had he not acted when he did.

"The officers in charge had disappeared. The people were in a highly excitable condition, and what had been only confusion was rapidly developing into a riot … With the assistance of two young Russian officers, and by assuming an authority I did not have, I got a 'death battalion' to throw a cordon around the town, establish patrols and restore some semblance of order."

The Death Battalion was comprised mostly of women. This courageous group of volunteers became "shock troops" that Joe was able to deploy to fight the Germans long enough for the soldiers to flee Tarnopol and re-establish in a defensive line to the south. For a short, bloody period, the women vexed the enemy and when the last of the Russian army had left, Joe followed.

Tarnopol fell to the Germans on July 24, a day later, and Joe accepted the mantle of a hero when he got back to Mogilev. He now wore the Military Order of Stanislaus as a blooded soldier.

It was almost too much for the British Foreign Office to bear! They sent the Russian army headquarters a telegram, bluntly informing them they did not consider Joe as functioning in any official military capacity. It made no difference to the Russians. General Tickmenev had already asked Joe to serve with his compatriots after a final report to the ACE was submitted. Tickmenev wanted Joe to investigate the transportation system on the eastern side of Rumania where the Germans had penned more than a million Russian soldiers.

Joe agreed to help, went to Petrograd to file his ACE reports, and sent a confidential plea to the secretary of colonial affairs, Walter Long, asking for a promotion to general. "...a general here receives attention and homage from almost everybody, whereas they look with a certain amount of familiarity...upon a colonel and raise questions they otherwise would not think of."

By the time the British were apologizing for Joe, he was in Jassy, the provisional capital of Rumania.

At the end of August, one year earlier, Rumania had entered the war on the side of Britain. In return for their alliance, Rumania had Bukovina, Transylvania, and the Banat repatriated. France had agreed to supply arms and munitions, and Russia the military support in the field. The decision to enter the war in this way had been a difficult choice for Rumania's King Ferdinand. Ferdinand was related to the Hohenzollern house of the German Kaiser, and Germans owned many key industries in Rumania. A small, poor army led by an old and inexperienced commander defended Ferdinand's country. In battle, they had to contend with wily German Field Marshall August von Mackensen, and a former Chief of the German General Staff, Field Marshall Erich von Falkenhays.

When Joe arrived in Jassy, he did as always and immediately asked to see the highest British and Rumanian authorities in place. Suddenly another blizzard of telegrams descended on the War Office. The British ambassador in Jassy, Sir George Barclay, didn't know what was expected of him as far as this Canadian was concerned. Barclay, like Buchanan in Petrograd, was another of the old school courtly diplomats. A connoisseur of fine wine and rich food, he was an elegant man who believed he balanced a delicate diplomatic situation in Rumania. Both he and Buchanan were appalled by Joe's blunt manner and honestly spoken appraisals, and feared Joe was capable of destroying amiable relationships at the highest levels if the War Office didn't move to "restrict his sphere of action severely."

The Foreign Office moved as quickly as they could to put Joe under the thumb of a "real" officer in the form of General de Candolle. To say Joe and de Candolle didn't get along would be an understatement.

When the Yukoner arrived in Jassy from Odessa in his private railcar, he had to wait for de Candolle to arrive and took the time to inspect the area. What he found appalled him. The rail lines were in a complete muddle and nothing was moving. Angered by the situation, he verbally lashed de Candolle when the two met, laying the blame for the situation on the military engineer's shoulders. De Candolle never officially complained about the insubordination, but privately called Joe an upstart colonial and military inferior who was a troublesome interloper.

Without permission, Joe ordered immediate changes in the running of the railway. He demanded that shipments be prioritized. Food first, the injured second, and military stores last. He evicted refugees who were using railcars as their homes and pushed the rolling stock into service. He had particularly bad parts of the railway line repaired and had both the Russian and Rumanian military hopping to his command. He cabled

London asking for ships to move cargo to starving troops by water instead of rail in the Danube River delta.

As Joe continued to bark orders, de Candolle fumed at all the insult Joe was causing to his reputation as leader. Once again the Foreign Office tried to rein him in, and once again, Joe foiled them by leaving Rumania on September 18 to return to Russian headquarters.

The British were beside themselves with worry. A telegram from the British ambassador in Jassy described Joe as "a man who was anxious to work independently." In poorly disguised frustration, the ambassador told his superiors that Joe "seemed to be a man not easily amenable to control of any kind." Because Joe was not actually in the military, no one knew from whom he was to take orders. Apparently, Joe didn't think it was de Candolle.

The confusion suited him just fine but the powers in Whitehall were livid. In October, the War Office tried to officially recall the civilian, but Joe now had a powerful group of friends in Russia. With the British screaming for the Canadian's removal from the theatre of war, the Russians happily attached him to their General Staff.

Joe was appointed by Stavka to organize the purchase of provisions for Russian troops stationed in Bessarabia, Rumania. He recommended a plan to Stavka that outlined the financing required, and he asked the ACE to do the purchasing.

Suddenly, even the Rumanian government was beginning to ask who this mysterious man of action was and what authority he wielded on behalf of the British war machine.

All the British ambassador could do was shrug. Joe had come to him asking for permission to write to the prime minister! Later, Joe even asked Buchanan to clarify just what the War Office saw as his position and promotion, and would the War Office kindly supply him some men so he could get something done?

"Tell me what I am to do," Buchanan telegrammed the Foreign Office plaintively. He wheedled to his superiors that Joe and Britain's General de Candolle didn't get along. De Candolle would issue orders to Joe and Joe would ignore them or refuse to follow direction. Worse than that, the Russians were adamant to have Joe continue helping them, and the Americans, who didn't get along with de Candolle either, were speaking up in support of the Russians.

Joe's presence had become a huge throbbing sore thumb to the British. When the Russian minister of foreign affairs telegrammed Whitehall to tell them they didn't want to see trouble erupt between the Americans and de Candolle by having Joe recalled, the Foreign Office staff were literally pulling their hair out. They obviously had no control over the man and neither, it seemed, did the War Office. In desperation to see their will done, they contacted Major General Sir. S.C. Mewburn, the minister of militia in Canada, pleading with him to recall Joe. They intimated a suspicion that Joe was so active in organizing supplies in Rumania because he was secretly taking commissions on what he ordered.

The War Office wrote to Canadian headquarters bluntly telling Ottawa that Joe's presence in Russia amounted to "a source of embarrassment."

Chapter 4
Instilling Order

Suspicions about Joe's honesty couldn't have been more unfounded. In fact, he argued against American corporate subterfuge to gain control over the civilian railway system. He'd left his mining interests in the hands of his son and focussed all his attention on the war effort. He ignored the legal morass with Granville Mining to concentrate fully on his Russian assignments now that he was virtually in charge of the military-zone railways from Petrograd to Odessa.

Joe continued his forceful and significant role advising the Russian army, going so far as to talk the

Russian commanders out of a plan to withdraw troops from Rumania. If the troops were to stay, the commanders said, they had to be fed, and the railway system had to be put in order before that could happen. If Joe could manage that Herculean feat, the troops, they agreed, could stay.

Joe rushed to Rumania on a special train to do what he could. He found that the British had decided to disassociate themselves from him, and that put the Rumanians in a tizzy. The Yukon miner, who'd faced far easier threats in bone chilling blizzards than this sudden cold shoulder from Whitehall, wrote to Barclay.

> *My position vis-à-vis your government, insofar as my work in Russia is concerned, is that I am a born British subject doing my best to help win this war and as such assumed that I was entitled to the assistance of its representatives and agents, all of whom are, presumably, at the present moment engaged in the same occupation.*
>
> *In Russia I have received the most courteous and considerate treatment, and every possible assistance from the British minister at Petrograd, the British military mission here, and from General Poole's office in Petrograd.*
>
> *I have not had any dealings with any other*

British agents except General de Candolle of whom I cannot speak so highly, but as I have no sort of connection with either himself or his mission I have naturally treated the matter as entirely personal and attached no importance to it.

It is, I think, unfortunate that your attitude in informing them that you had to "disassociate" yourself from my sphere of activities has frightened the Rumanian government into refusing to accept the help offered them, and which my position enabled me to render, and I only hope that the assistance they are accepting along the same lines may be effective and sufficient.

Joe wrote that he was willing to help if the Rumanians changed their minds, and concluded by telling the ambassador "all of the works advised by me in connection with the lines of transport leading to Rumania has [sic] been adopted and there is now no danger of any famine there on account of the lack of transport."

Even if the British and the Rumanians had now turned away from Joe, the Russians were still happily engaging his service. In Jassy, the general who commanded the Russian forces in the area sent him to the front with the duty to reorganize the construction work of the railway in Bessarabia, a region between Rumania and Russia. Joe took up permanent residence on the tracks in an ornate, up-to-date saloon car that gave him handy access to the work being done.

Up to that point in time, Joe had seen a Russian army that was loyal to its old guard officers, but the revolution had a deep impact on that loyalty. He began to realize that more Russian troops were leaning towards Bolshevik beliefs. The Bolsheviks had managed to garner support from the Cossacks, and in the city of Mogilev particularly, they were fomenting trouble with the help of German interests.

The British had assigned a secret agent (code named I-K8) to watch the Germans. The agent, Captain George Hill, used a position as a staff officer with the British Artillery Mission as his cover. He had been recruited to army intelligence in Salonika. The son of a British businessman, he had been born and raised in Russia and spoke the language fluently.

On one night in October, Hill was attacked by one of the German agents. With a sword he had hidden in his walking stick, Hill managed to kill his assailant, and afterwards stumbled his way into the Bristol Hotel and Joe's arms. The Canadian, a little bemused, assisted Hill, and from that night on became one of the secret agent's closest friends.

Not long after their dramatic introduction Joe met with an excited Hill in Stavka. The agent told Joe that German agitators had helped to organize a meeting of military units and that they were attempting to rouse the Russians into demanding the expulsion of all Allied military from the area. Hill asked Joe to attend the meeting and speak to the Russians. Perhaps, because of the respect he'd earned, they might listen to him.

When Joe arrived, the meeting organizers tried to have him ejected. However, the unruly crowd included a number in favour of his presence and they called for a vote. Joe suspected that within a few seconds the nays would win, and he and his translator, Hill, would have to leave. With Hill at his side, Joe entered the near riotous meeting, striding forward with his old boxer's "on the attack" style. He moved through the crowd, ignoring the curses being spat by the German agitators, and leapt to the stage.

Though his words were being translated, it was clear he was speaking to the patriotic heart of the men in the crowd, who respectfully quieted to listen. He started by telling them of Canada and his travails in the North. Then he drew parallels with Russia. He reminded them of their history, and of the courage of their victories against the heaviest of odds. Russians, he told them, never retreat.

"You are men, not sheep," he shouted. "I order you to act as men." The crowd, by this time hooked on every word, erupted into applause. "Long live the Allies!" they shouted. "Down with the Germans."

The mob had turned into a cheering audience, proving one more time that Joe had an almost intuitive sense of what to say to men in times of stress. His boldness seemed always to strike a positive chord.

When the Bolsheviks led a second revolt in October and overthrew the government, Joe's intuition was proven one more time.

Learning of the Bolshevik action, Joe and Hill rushed to Petrograd and with his bluster, Joe managed to gain an audience with a leader of the October Revolution. The Petrograd Revolutionary Committee president, Comrade A. Joffe, welcomed Joe and told him the new government was eager to continue retaining his efforts to maintain supplies to the southwestern front. Joffe also asked Joe if he would help immediately with a rail traffic snarl that had closed the Moscow Junction to all traffic.

At the time, anti-Bolsheviks manned the technical boards at the railway. They had purposely caused the snarl as their way of sabotage. When street fighting in Moscow added to the mess so that no shipments of food got in or out of the city for a six-day period, the new

Bolshevik government was in fear of collapse.

On November 17, it was reported that food supplies to the southwestern front were down to a nine-day stock and the army was near starvation. In Rumania, the situation was worse, with less than a week of food supplies left, and in Moscow, as many as 10,000 cars were bottled up in the railway snarl. The Bolsheviks were willing to accept any help they could get.

Joffe gave Joe permission to go anywhere and take any action he thought necessary to remedy the situation. For Joe's part, he'd seen the ineptitude rampant in the previous government and was not aware of the brutalities of the Revolution. Until he learned that the Bolsheviks intended on pulling out of the war, he supported their efforts to ease the plight of the Russian people.

The Bolsheviks had seized and imprisoned General Manikovski, an army commander loyal to the government. Joe asked for Manikovski's release to help clear the Moscow chaos. When Joe got to Moscow, the street fighting between Bolsheviks and anti-Bolsheviks was still rampant. The Bolsheviks (also called the Red Army) had 50,000 men fighting a determined White Army (the faction loyal to the existing government) of only 10,000.

With Hill as his translator, Joe met with N. Muralov, the Bolshevik commander in the district, and was soon given complete authority over the rail lines in the region. Notices were posted that all drivers and labourers were required to report for work under Joe's command the next day. If they failed to do so, six of their group would be picked out and shot.

Joe was ready and willing to give the execution squad the order. He took to his task with zeal, often removing his own uniform, grabbing a pick, and joining the workers on the rail line reconstruction. It was unheard of for an officer to do such a thing, and the workers were both bewildered and awed. The Canadian seemed bent on proving he was a better man than any who served for him, and they worked doubly hard to prove him wrong. When they slacked, Joe would climb atop a railway car and with the aid of translators, push the men on with jokes, cheers, and songs.

The threats of execution and Joe's incessant urging got the Moscow rail snarl cleared in just two days. In some instances Joe had resorted to extreme measures. If engines were blocking the line and had been sabotaged, he simply had them pushed off the track. Empty cars were pushed off sidings into open fields as well.

Joe and Hill returned to Stavka on November 15. Joe was given the private railcar formerly used by Russia's Dowager Empress Mother Marie Feodorovna as his own, and the two Allied officers travelled from

Stavka to Petrograd in baronial comfort.

The Rumanian government saw the almost miraculous transformation of the railway system in Moscow and suddenly asked for Joe's assistance. On November 25, Count Di'Amandi, the Rumanian ambassador in Petrograd, formally signed the papers that commissioned Joe to "procure supplies and equipment" for the Rumanian people.

Joe went to work organizing supplies for a week and then turned his railcar towards Mogilev. When he arrived, he found the earth shaking beneath the Russian officers there. Commander in Chief General Dukhonin had been ordered by Lenin and Stalin to begin negotiations for peace with the Central Powers, but he had refused.

Dukhonin was a mild, honourable man who believed that the agreement the provisional government had made with the Allies not to negotiate a separate peace should be supported. Lenin's council of commissars' answer was to send N.V. Krilenko, the sailor who had led the people's revolutionary uprising in Petrograd, to replace Dukhonin as commander. Instead of fleeing, Dukhonin stayed at his post until December 3, and that afternoon, a mob of sailors from the Baltic fleet seized him.

As Joe's railway car was being pulled into the

Mogilev rail yards, he witnessed the mob dragging Dukhonin towards Krilenko's staff railway car. The crowd was screaming for Dukhonin's execution, but Krilenko tried to calm them with refusals. Joe watched helplessly as Dukhonin was pushed from Krilenko's rear platform into the mob. They tossed him into the air and fired at the flying body. As he dropped, they readied their bayonets and impaled him. His body was kicked, beaten with rifle butts, and then discarded in a refuse shed, a bloody, broken corpse.

Joe waited for the mob to rush towards Mogilev, where the thugs were intent on murdering Dukhonin's family, and then he ran to Krilenko's railway car. In a fury, he verbally whipped the new commander, calling him a coward unfit to lead, then demanded Krilenko promise to see that Dukhonin was given an honourable burial.

What Joe had witnessed that afternoon soured his opinion of the Bolsheviks forever. In future, though he worked for them to achieve his own ends, his secret desire was to see the new government ripped from power in the same heartless way as they had gained it.

Joe was in Jassy by Christmas Day 1917, tired and unhappy. He'd learned, belatedly, that his mining company had been placed in receivership back in the Yukon over the dispute with Granville Mining, and he'd just completed the most harrowing week of his life.

First, he had gone to Moscow to gather food and clothing for the Rumanian army, as the Rumanian ambassador in Petrograd had requested of him. There he had accomplished a feat that would make him a hero in the beleaguered little country, as well as in Russia.

While he was in Moscow, the Rumanian consul-general and representatives of the National Bank had approached Joe. They asked him to transport "the archives of the foreign office, some paper notes and other valuables" to Jassy, along with the other supplies. Of course, Joe had agreed.

The Rumanian crown jewels, national bullion treasury, and archives had been moved to Moscow more than a year before, when Rumania had declared war on the Central Powers. The move had been a precaution against the treasure's loss should the Austro-German army overrun the country.

Procuring the food and clothing supplies for the Rumanian army was a delicate task. It required deception to get into the Russian warehouses, as well as the assistance of middle-rank Russian officers, but Joe had managed to gather 155 freight cars worth of supplies.

To get the Rumanian crown jewels, the equivalent of £4 million in Rumanian currency, £25 million worth of gold reserves, and the nation's archives aboard the same train took a lot more Irish luck and Yukon moxy.

With the empowering letter written by Muralov (the man who had given Joe complete command of the railway workers in Moscow), the Canadian was able to gain discreet access to the Kremlin vaults. He managed to spirit some of the crown jewels, the currency, and the archives from the Kremlin to the railway station, where his supply train waited.

Perhaps Joe was allowed to take the treasure because no one actually thought he could get away. Or perhaps it was the manner in which he commanded the warehouse guards. Regardless, he and Hill were able to first move the jewels to a Red Cross building and then stuff them into 31 small and 5 large Red Cross containers. After some argument with the Russian charged with maintaining Joe's personal railcar, the baskets, boxes, and containers were squeezed into four of its sleeping compartments.

The treasure saloon was hitched to the first westbound train, and as it eased out of the station, Joe was told there was a good possibility it would be ambushed 80 kilometres from Moscow. Joe took the warning seriously. He had only six men aboard to defend the cargo. Riding atop the railway cars, pistols in hand, Hill and Joe began a perilous 2400-kilometre journey across southern Russia.

Sure enough, when they reached the appointed distance, the train pulled into a small station and made an unscheduled stop. Joe alighted from the train to inspect his surroundings and found several shadowy figures attempting to uncouple the treasure car from the engine. He leapt upon them, knocking one out and sending the others scattering in fear.

With hollow apologies offered by the stationmaster, the car was rejoined and the train quickly resumed its journey. Joe and his men had to travel through the Ukraine, which was embroiled in a growing civil strife between Bolsheviks and Ukrainian nationalists. At Briansk, the train ran a gauntlet of bullets between the two factions who were shooting at each other in the station.

On the second night of the journey, a wild blaze prompted an unscheduled stop. Near the railway right-of-way, a vodka distillery was burning out of control. The train's occupants cheerfully relieved the building of as much of the liquor as they could carry, and the train then carried on. The group made steady progress until the next afternoon, when a mounted Bolshevik detachment stopped the train. Joe donned his uniform and met the commissar in charge of the detachment. He lied claiming that the railcar was owned by a foreign embassy and therefore not within the boundaries of the

A map of Eastern Europe in 1914–18 showing the route
of the daring Rumanian crown jewels rescue

commissar's authority. Somehow, he got through.

About 200 kilometres from Kiev, the train ran out of fuel and water in an isolated forested area covered in snow so deep the drifts beside the tracks reached to the men's armpits. Joe's first trek out of Dawson in January had prepared him for such weather. Spotting a group of peasants, he commandeered them into forming a chain gang to collect firewood, while Hill guarded the train and melted snow for water.

As they resumed their journey, they encountered whole regions of the Ukraine under the smoky pall of revolutionary upheaval. At Vapnyarka, they had the most dangerous of all their encounters.

A gun battery commanded by Bolshevik officers stopped the train as a front of foul weather began to descend on the city. It could have been a disaster, but Joe smiled at the heavily armed force and then studied the sky. Rather than put up a pointless fight against the much larger Bolshevik group, he decided to host a party for them using the vodka that had been purloined from the distillery. With rousing song, and tea spiked liberally with his secret ingredient, Joe had his adversaries singing and dancing themselves into a stupor within hours. As the storm hit the town, Joe and Hill rapidly moved to sever the telephone and telegraph lines to stop the Bolsheviks from warning their compatriots further along the tracks. They then located an idling engine and at gunpoint, forced the engineer and stoker to hook up the treasure cars and quietly move out of town.

The weather was so foul that the engineer was operating the train blindly. All seemed well for 20 minutes. Then the engineer spotted a blockade across the track. As he eased off the throttle, Joe pushed him aside. He figured the momentum of the heavy locomotive would make fast work of the hastily piled timber, and he was right. At full throttle, with the momentum of tons of treasure pushing even more speed out of the engine, they rammed the blockade sending Bolsheviks, timber, and snow flying in every direction.

Without further complication, Joe and Hill reached Odessa and finally the capital of Jassy on Christmas Eve, four days after they'd set out. To personally express her gratitude, Queen Marie of Rumania gave an audience to the two adventurous interlopers.

Marie was considered to be the most beautiful royal in Europe. She was Joe's junior by eight years, having been born in England in 1875 as the second child of Alfred, Duke of Edinburgh and Grand Duchess Marie Alexandrovna. Granddaughter of England's Queen Victoria, Marie had been married at the age of 17 to the Hohenzollern crown prince of Rumania.

Ferdinand I, nicknamed "Nando" by Marie,

ascended to the throne in 1914, so Marie had only served a few years as a monarch when she first met Joe. She was a romantic, almost soppy woman. She had a tendency to over-dramatize every event in her life, colouring it with a self-centred, almost mawkish sentimental sheen. Joe's audience made an impressive impact upon her.

Afterwards, on March 7, 1918, she described the meeting. "...I had a busy day. I had to receive a very interesting Englishman, a certain Colonel Boyle who is working for us in Russia trying to better our situation. A very curious fascinating sort of man, who is frightened of nothing and who, by his extraordinary force of will and fearlessness gets through everywhere. The real type English adventurer books are written about. Alas I could not talk with him half enough..."

Marie found Joe to be a refreshing interlude in her busy day. His eyes, she said, were deep blue and keen, "sometimes even fierce." He had a grip of steel but hands that were "refined." She invited him to a celebratory Christmas party, but Joe declined. Instead, the next day found him quietly enjoying a well-deserved dinner alone while Queen Marie and King Ferdinand entertained Hill and the British Embassy staff at a ball.

Chapter 5
A Secret Life

I t seemed too much to ask to gain a few days of reprieve from Whitehall's heckling. The British still wanted to see Joe removed from Rumania so that they could re-establish their diplomatic balance without his independent interference.

On January 26, 1918, a cipher telegram was sent from Whitehall to the Duke of Devonshire, Governor General of Canada. Colonial Secretary Walter Long, supposedly one of Joe's friends, had prepared the message.

"Boyle, since his arrival has negotiated directly

with Russian authorities without reference to either British ambassador or British military attaché. His activities extended to Rumania as well as Russia and he has been dealing not only with railway matters but also with political, financial, military and food questions. He has evinced utmost repugnance to co-operate with Inter-Allied representatives and refuses to recognize any party. His independent action has caused much trouble to Allied Railway Mission and his presence in Russia has been the source of constant embarrassment to British representative..."

Whitehall wanted the Governor General to issue an official recall for Joe. The message was passed to the prime minister, and from him to the minister of defence, and from him to the cabinet. It rolled back and forth through Ottawa like a pinball. After five days it was decided that such an order would be made, but the cabinet had no idea how they would get the order to Joe, much less if he would listen.

The Rumanian government officials had other ideas. Though Joe might have reasonably expected a furlough from his duties so he could go to London and defend himself in the Granville litigation, it wasn't to be.

For some time, food supplies had failed to make it to Jassy. The situation was almost desperate and would soon reach starvation level. Even the palace was suffering. The ball the queen had hosted to honour Hill and the British at Christmas had been meagre. She had served the diplomats soup with shreds of horsemeat and cabbage for flavour, some boiled maize, and a single slice of heavy black bread that they had washed down with a vinegar-like wine or coffee that had been made from dried acorns. Hardly a royal banquet.

Besides the privations of war, Bolshevik agitators had prevented food shipments from reaching General Tscherbatchef and his 4th Russian army at Jassy. The Bolsheviks hoped that hungry stomachs would foment revolution among the soldiers faster than political speeches. Tscherbatchef asked Joe to inspect conditions and rectify matters if he could. One Russian corps particularly was singled out for Joe's special attention. Agitators there were calling for soldiers to kill their officers and to loot the countryside.

Joe did a review and quickly made some decisions. Because the men were starving, he had 50 percent of the army horses slaughtered for meat. There was enough feed for the remaining horses to last the winter, so the fodder trains were put to different use. Then he had the agitators identified and imprisoned. To Joe it was quick, easy work, but the swiftness of his actions pleased Tscherbatchef immensely. He immediately decorated Joe with the Order of Vladimir, Fourth Class.

The Rumanian government also noted the quick resolution of the crisis. By then, the government was far more worried about a war with the new Russian regime than it was about the Central Powers taking the country. Because he felt Joe had friends within the Bolshevik ranks, Rumanian Prime Minister Bratiano asked Joe to help broker a resolution. Bratiano was willing to give up Bessarabia, territory that King Ferdinand had regained from Russia when he had declared war on Austria and Germany, in exchange for peace with the Bolsheviks.

Bratiano was also willing to facilitate the withdrawal of Russian forces from Rumania, and in turn he promised to withdraw Rumanian troops from Bessarabia. Proposing this deal meant that Joe would have to travel to Petrograd, but he was quite willing to do that for secret reasons of another kind.

For some time Joe had been operating as a double agent. On the surface he was working with the Bolsheviks to aid their cause, but he was also using his time in Russia to gather information for the benefit of the Allies. As early as October 1917, Joe had secretly agreed to spy for the Allies and organize an intelligence service to offset German activities in Russia. His participation was so confidential that only a handful of embassy personnel, and his friend Hill, knew what he was doing. In Jassy he met with General Henri Berthelot, the commander of a French military advisory mission who had a plan to stall any Bolshevik occupation of Bessarabia and the Don Basin.

Joe was instructed to use his Bolshevik authority to "drift locomotives from the North to the South of Russia, and create as much disorder and confusion in the railway system as possible."

With Hill at his side, Joe took his private railway car to Moscow and renewed his acquaintance with Muralov. Simultaneously, Rumanian soldiers corralled every Bolshevik they could find in their country and confiscated their weapons. The Bolsheviks reacted in a similar fashion. As a result, the countryside around Jassy became a hodgepodge of conflicting control. Each railway station, for example, had both a Russian and a Rumanian commandant, which inevitably led to chaos.

Joe discovered that Muralov, in the weeks since they'd last worked together, had been placed in charge of 11 districts around Moscow. Muralov agreed to accompany Joe to Petrograd and organize a meeting with Bolshevik War Commissar Podvoiski at which Joe might further arrange a meeting with Trotsky, the foreign minister. He planned to present Prime Minister Bratiano's offer to Trotsky.

When he got to Petrograd, Joe first tried to meet with Rumanian ambassador di'Amandi to inform him of Bratiano's plan. He soon discovered the diplomat had been arrested in retaliation for the Russian arrests in Rumania. At Joe's urging, diplomatic pressure was applied from other countries and di'Amandi was released. However. instead of participating in the peace talks Joe was sent to arrange, the ambassador fearfully fled to Finland.

When that happened, Joe's negotiations turned sour. He was supposed to talk with Trotsky, but Trotsky was in Brest-Liovsk attempting to negotiate his own peace accord for the Bolsheviks with the Central Powers. The foreign minister was not expected to return until January 18. In desperation, Joe met with Trotsky's nephew, Zalkind.

Zalkind was a challenge even for Joe's gregarious Irish blarney. The man was a hunchback with a vicious nature who hated the English and despised Rumanians. He happily told Joe that he was opposed to the Rumanian proposals, and that he had serious doubts about Joe's intentions. "Starve Rumania into revolution," was Zalkind's answer. No exchange was to occur and no mercy missions of food would be allowed.

Zalkind perhaps sensed that Joe was not quite what he seemed. If so, he was more right than he could have imagined.

Joe had been privately recruiting 10 spies for his

network while working for the Bolsheviks. Each of the carefully picked men then also recruited 10, and they 10 more. The commanders of each unit reported to, and took orders from, the man who had recruited them. In this way, Joe was able to give his orders to the whole spy network by speaking to only 10 individuals.

"The work laid out for them by me," Joe reported to General Ballard at the British Embassy in Jassy, "is to get employment in repair shops of railways and coal mines — to carefully retard all work — 'accidentally' break or do away with spare parts of machines difficult or impossible to replace particularly on imported locomotives and pumps; strip thread on fixed bolts and whenever possible do anything to a locomotive or pump that will cause breakage."

It was Joe who gave the men orders to blow up bridges and supply depots. It was this smiling "friend" of the Bolsheviks who told his men to spread propaganda about how the Germans intended to turn Russia into a colony of slave labourers.

By the time he met with Zalkind, Joe controlled 44 units of spies with 484 members in his network. In spite of the screams by Whitehall to have Joe recalled, Britain was in fact financing his effort, as was France. The enormous sums of £10 million and 100 million French Francs were at Joe's disposal. Joe already knew that

Trotsky's peace-making efforts in Brest-Litovsk would fail as he faced Zalkind in Petrograd. His men had already convinced a controlling number of Bolshevik leaders to refuse to abide by any treaty.

It must have tickled the Canadian to see the Bolsheviks, Muralov, and Podvoiski argue so enthusiastically with Zalkind in his favour, vouching for his character as a man who could get things accomplished where all others had failed.

Muralov and Podvoiski urged Zalkind to give Joe further authority to travel south and try to increase the output of coal in the Donnetz Basin for the Bolshevik cause. This was another stroke of luck for Joe, for he already had a network of secret agents in the area and needed to speak to them. Zalkind finally acceded and Joe was asked to investigate the transportation difficulties in the south. He was given permission to meet with Antonov Ovsenko, a member of the Bolshevik government who at the time was commander of the southern front.

At the request of Sir Francis Lindley, the acting British chargé d'affaires in Petrograd, Joe also agreed to take along a stack of mail pouches and two British officers bound for the Caucasus. Curiously, while the British government was officially howling for Joe's recall and secretly paying him to spy, Joe was also serving the king as a postman.

Hostilities between Russia and Rumania continued to escalate while Joe hurried about on his mission of "peace." By the end of January, the Bolsheviks had severed all relations with Rumania. Rumanian officers had been forced out of Russia and the Bolsheviks had formed the Supreme Autonomous Colloquium (SAC) in Odessa to regulate Russian/Rumanian affairs.

Joe tracked down Antonov as he'd been instructed and got a good hearing, but he was informed that the Rumanian peace proposal had to be presented to Dr. Christian Rakovsky, the new SAC chairman in Sebastopol, Ukraine.

Antonov did provide Joe with travelling papers and an agreement to supply food to Rumanian civilians if members of the SAC authorized it.

On his way to see Rakovsky, Joe stopped in the Donnetz Basin, as he'd pledged to Zalkind he would do. With quick recommendations he closed non-essential industries that were using up the coal and oil supplies and had former railway officials who'd been dismissed by the Bolsheviks put back to work. Two weeks later, available coal and fuel supplies climbed by 47 percent. Again, to the Bolsheviks, Joe was a hero.

He left the Donnetz Basin in a rush, dying to give the Rumanian prime minister his good news about a peace treaty, but his train was soon stopped in Kherson, a city in the Ukraine. The British consul there told Joe that the German secret service had somehow learned what he was up to and was trying to sabotage the mission's progress by spreading rumours that the British had made a secret deal with Turkey. The German agitators were claiming that the British fleet would soon be attacking Rumania. It was a ludicrous tale. Wary nonetheless, Joe continued to Sebastopol on his guard, but he wasn't prepared for what awaited him.

At the Sebastopol station, sailor mutineers led by a clubfooted man named Speiro, who was certain Joe was the vanguard for the British fleet, surrounded his train. Joe did his best to convince Speiro otherwise, brandishing Antonov's signed permissions to travel. Then he invited eight of the mob into his railway car. With ample food and drink, he calmly explained the German strategy, pointing out how the Russians were being made to look like fools. The mob left screaming insults at the Germans with the intention of destroying the pro-German newspaper that had published the false propaganda.

Speiro insisted that Joe and Hill, now his fast friends, visit the Crimean War battlefields and meet each of the revolutionary committees in the Black Sea fleet.

It took time, and was a pleasant interlude, but Joe doubted dealing with Rakovsky, an erudite and well-educated man, would be as easy.

Chapter 6
The "Saviour of Rumania"

Joe finally reached Odessa, where Rakovsky was now based, on February 20, 1918. Upon his arrival, he dived immediately into the political miasma. With the Rumanian Order of the Crown medal — bestowed by Marie for his treasure train episode — dangling from a blue ribbon around his neck, Joe set up meetings with Rakovsky and the Rumcherod, the Supreme Council of the region.

Rakovsky quickly confirmed Antonov's agreement on food, but added a proviso that the Rumanians must stop all military activity against Russia. Then they began the peace negotiations. They went on for two days and through the night of a third before the delegates signed a final draft. In a staff car provided by Rakovsky, Joe urgently charged on to Bessarabia and then to Jassy.

To Joe's dismay, the Rumanian government was not at all eager to sign the treaty with the Bolsheviks. Pro-German factions had been pushing the government to pen a deal with the Central Powers instead, and no one seemed at all concerned about the five dozen Rumanian notables who had been seized by the Russians in Odessa as hostages.

The exchange of prisoners was a hard won part of the peace treaty Joe had hammered out with Rakovsky and the Rumcherod, but unless the treaty was signed, the effort had been wasted. While Joe waited tensely for the cabinet decision, his frustration levels soared. No one, it seemed, could get through to him. Not even King Ferdinand.

When the Rumanian king invited Joe to an audience to discuss the treaty process, the Canadian curtly told the king's messenger that he was too busy. If the king wanted to talk to him so badly he could use a telephone.

Everyone expected the Germans to advance quickly on the Rumanian border, thanks to a duplicitous agreement made with the Russians that allowed 130 troop trucks to reach the Danube River even while Russian leaders were talking peace with Joe.

Queen Marie overlooked Joe's faux pas with the king, and in the next few days invited him to meet with her privately at least three times. She saw something truly unique in his character that attracted her.

The attraction was cemented on March 9. With the Germans advancing, the Allied missions decided to leave Jassy for fear they might be caught behind German lines. The last of their departures occurred on that miserably rainy night. Marie had insisted on saying farewell to the Allies personally, which angered the pro-German factions in her court. She was sombre and heartbroken at the thought of occupation and sat alone in tears when the last Allied group left.

At the doorway to the reception hall a sudden shadow appeared and then Joe, soaked to the skin, came forward. He'd been waiting in the rain for the final departures.

"Have you come to see me?" she asked.

Joe shook his head and quietly told her no. "I have come to help you. And my God, woman, do you need help."

Joe stayed with Marie in the reception hall to offer support while she wept in his arms. Later in her diary she described an "irresistible sympathy" that formed between them.

"We understood each other from the first moment we clasped hands, as though we had never been strangers," she wrote.

"I tried to let myself be steeled by the man's relentless energy, tried to absorb some of the quiet force which emanates from him. I poured out my heart to him in those hours.... I do not know all that I told him, the memory is a blur, but I made a clean breast of all my grief and when he left me and I said that everyone was forsaking me, he answered very quietly 'but I don't' and the grip of his hand was strong as iron."

After three days of ruminating, the Rumanian cabinet finally signed Joe's negotiated treaty, and before the Canadian left, Marie reminded him that 70 prisoners still needed to be rescued. Joe made a solemn promise he would look after her subjects.

The Rumanian cabinet turned to Joe as their representative, calling on him to finalize the peace agreement. To do so he was dispatched in a two-seater plane supplied by Berthelot, the French commander for whom he was also secretly spying.

Joe landed in Odessa on March 10, 1918, two days before the expected takeover by the Germans. The peace treaty was duly signed, and historically became the first to have been negotiated during World War I.

The "Saviour of Rumania"

As agreed, the 70 high-ranking Rumanian prisoners in Odessa would be allowed to leave the walled fortress of Turma prison. On March 12, they would be exchanged for 400 Russians being held in Rumania, along with the safe passage of 100,000 more unarmed Russian soldiers waiting for orders from Russia.

One of the Rumanian prisoners was a naval commander named Bruno Pantazzi, and he was married to a Canadian. Ethel Greening Pantazzi had come from Hamilton, Ontario, to be with her Rumanian husband. She sought out Joe to learn the specifics of the transfer. Joe told her the prisoners were to board a special train and depart under guard, and that she could accompany them. Early on the morning of the evacuation, however, Ethel received an anonymous call.

Rakovsky had discovered that the German army had been permitted to march across a part of Rumania to do battle with the Russians, soundly defeating them at Birsula. He planned to exact a small vengeance. He ordered his Death Battalion of zealots to move the prisoners to a ship that was headed to the Crimea instead of Rumania. Ethel hurriedly searched for Joe and relayed the news.

Unable to believe that Rakovsky would betray their deal, Joe went to the docks to see for himself. When he discovered the prisoners were indeed there, he immediately went to the Rumanian royal yacht, the *Stefan-cel-Mare,* which had been seized by the Bolsheviks to become the headquarters of the Death Battalion. There he learned Rakovsky had left Odessa, and had taken all the prisoners' valuables with him.

The man left in charge, named Dichescu, was 16 years younger than Joe and a far cry from the cultured, intelligent Rakovsky. He looked to Joe as though he had not had a bath for some time and was in a constant state of unease, furtively checking over his shoulder for enemies that were not there.

Dichescu listened to Joe's argument that Rakovsky had agreed to the prisoner exchange in an official treaty. Joe demanded Dichescu keep Rakovsky's word as an honourable Bolshevik. The powerful-looking Canadian must have been an intimidating verbal opponent, because though Dichescu had no proof that the agreement was still in force, he deferred to three Supreme Autonomous Colloquium members who dutifully sealed the release with their own signatures.

But Joe could not get the Death Battalion soldiers themselves to release the prisoners. Neither could Dichescu. In an act of desperation aimed at delaying their departure, Joe insisted the prisoners be paraded on the dock so he could count them all. Once there the guards immediately ordered them back on board the boat. Confusion erupted as a few tried to escape. Two were shot, but seven others succeeded in their bid for freedom.

Joe exploded with anger. While the Rumanians cowered, diving for cover, he charged up the gangplank and attacked the firing soldiers with bare-fisted rage, ignoring the danger from a rifle-shot at close range. "Why are you shooting on my prisoners?" he screamed, knocking over the soldiers as though they were bowling pins.

Fearing for the lives of the rest, Joe refused to leave the ship and was among the remaining prisoners as the *Imperator Trajan* steamed away from the dock. The prisoners were forced into one large room and given tin cabbage to share as their food on the journey.

For three days the ship battled storms as it steamed from port to port along the Black Sea coastline until finally docking at the Ukraine city of Feodosiya with its starving and thirsty cargo.

Feodosiya was in chaos. Residents and Bolsheviks were rioting. Bloody mayhem was everywhere. The Death Battalion guards led the ragged prisoners from the ship through the street battles to a cholera hospital where they were to await further instructions. It wasn't the healthiest of surroundings, but at least the men could finally get some rest on the straw-covered floor.

Joe noted the look of fear and resignation in the prisoners' eyes and reacted to it with bravado. He calmly removed his boots and took the time to wash his socks. Barefoot, his uniform pants rolled up to his knees, he wandered the hospital offering the men simple words of encouragement.

Immediate execution seemed a remote possibility. But when the British vice-consul in Feodosiya told Joe that two sympathetic members of the ship's crew were claiming the Death Battalion intended on marching the prisoners to an ammunition shed and blowing it up, he decided it was not the time to take chances.

When there was a lull in the street fighting, Joe worked with the vice-consul to organize an escape. With 10 Chinese soldiers from the Bolshevik International Battalion following his command, Joe succeeded in cutting telephone lines, and then quietly marched the prisoners to another boat, the *Chernomore*. The vice-consul had succeeded in bribing the captain with 150,000 rubles. As the prisoners reached the gangway of the *Chernomore,* two members of the Death Squad spotted them and began asking questions. Joe claimed he had permission to move the men and invited the Bolsheviks aboard the boat to show the documents. Once they were on the ship, he had them locked in a cabin.

The *Chernomore* slipped out of Feodosiya before

the Death Battalion could react, but the prisoners' real problems were only beginning. At the mouth of the Danube they encountered the German navy.

Joe faced the enemy with his Irish blarney again, and somehow convinced the region commander, Field Marshal von Mackensen, that his was a mission of mercy. Von Mackensen, inclined to be generous, insisted that if he provided safe conduct, and if Joe was truly not engaged in an act of war, the Canadian should remove his uniform.

"Tell him that no German living will compel me to take off my uniform," Joe replied to the translator. "I carry a single-action Colt, and I am a man of my word. I promise to drill holes in the first German, be he General or Private, who lays violent hands on me."

Von Mackensen must have been impressed by Joe's patriotism and courage. Since this evidently was a mission of mercy, this man's clothing was not material. The Field Marshal shrugged and provided his permission for free passage to Jassy.

However, in Sulina, farther along the Danube, the Austrian commander who Joe found waiting for him didn't fall as easily for Joe's bluster. He refused to allow the boat to dock for the prisoner exchange. Von Mackensen had telegrammed his safe conduct permission ahead, but the Austrian refused to recognize the

German's authority. The *Chernomore* would have to anchor in mid-stream, Austrian Commander Wolff said, until he got Austrian orders. With indignant anger, Joe demanded the Austrian put his mutinous opinion in writing for the kaiser. The Austrian must have felt a pang or two of doubt, but he remained resolved.

The prisoner boat was moved into the river and to keep a wary eye on the suspicious shipload of men, the Austrian ordered his war ships to take position in front, behind, and on either side. He capped his distrust for the Canadian by having two seaplanes, with machine guns at the ready, fly patrol overhead. While this was going on, a Rumanian boat, filled with 100 Russian prisoners for the exchange, made its way to the Sulina dock.

Joe decided to rebel. He notified the Austrian that he was going to follow his orders to effect the prisoner transfer, and then sail regardless of the Austrian naval guns.

The next morning at 8 a.m., Joe put the Rumanian prisoners ashore at Sulina and got up steam on the *Chernomore*. He assigned a few of the crew to man a decrepit gun on the stern and again notified Wolff of his intention to force his way into harbour. Wolff responded by preparing his boats to fire on the ship. When Joe hadn't moved by 9:30, Wolff invited the Canadian to a meeting and informed him he'd been officially told that the exchange could indeed now occur.

Joe watched as the Russians were quickly moved aboard the *Chernomore*. It sailed immediately with the soldiers cheering and shouting their gratitude to the Bolshevik hero, Joe Boyle.

To get his Rumanian charges home, Joe hired a barge to transport them to the train station at Galatz. To Joe's dismay, there were no seats available on the train to Jassy except one reserved for him. He refused to leave the prisoners, telegraphed Jassy, and waited. Within two hours the train returned for them all.

When the group finally arrived in Jassy, Joe was given a hero's welcome. To the tears of Marie and hugs from Ferdinand, Joe was awarded the Star of Rumania and the Grand Cross. Newspapers hailed him as the "Saviour of Rumania." Crowds besieged him as he walked in the streets. The hostages hosted a special dinner at which one man named J. Lucasiwicz said Joe's actions were a sign of his "deep sympathy for the whole nation."

All Rumanians, Lucasiwicz said, "have been able to realize your qualities of great energy, courage, strength [and] will keep it in mind and ... transform it into the symbol of the creed that nations have the duty, and the power, to struggle until the last breath."

The Yukoner's conduct served to soften the official

British attitude towards him once London was notified of his successful rescue. Joe had made friends in both camps — with the Bolsheviks as Colonel Boylsheviki and with the Rumanians simply as Joe. Even Trotsky made official his admiring opinion of the Canadian. Strangely enough, neither London nor Ottawa joined in by recognizing him for the achievement.

Chapter 7
Feeding a Nation

Von Mackensen's pass to Jassy prevented Joe from crossing the German lines again back into Russia. When Joe asked the Rumanian government to intercede with the Germans, he was ignored. The impasse left him time to visit with Queen Marie on several occasions, riding horses in the countryside, attending church services, taking a brief holiday to Cotafanesti to visit a royal hunting lodge with her and others, and enjoying dinners in the royal summer palace. When two planes were turned over to his use by the Rumanian air force, however, Joe was able to maintain partial contact with his spy network. For the most part, May was a month of forced leisure.

In contrast, the first 10 days of June saw Joe at his most hyperactive. He flew and drove automobiles to several meetings, rarely remaining in a location for more than a few hours at a time. With Allied financing, Joe was busy buying any supplies he could in Bessarabia to cripple the German supply line.

During this time it seems likely the relationship between Joe and Queen Marie deepened and they became lovers. King Ferdinand had a reputation for his own dalliances. Perhaps Queen Marie felt freer to accept the Canadian's bold advances. He was a man of strong will and energy, and was definitely full-blooded. He made his own rules and probably didn't restrict himself with old-fashioned standards that denied him women of importance like Marie. He was a man who was obviously in love and she was a romantic who bestowed her affection towards him openly.

In their private hours, Joe and Queen Marie discussed the future of her nation. Joe told her his ideas for reform and urged her to improve the conditions of Rumanian peasants to forestall their own revolution. He was appalled at the burden of labour that peasant women had to bear and called upon Marie to promote a sharing of the workload by the men and the boys.

Queen Marie in native Rumanian costume

During the many evenings he spent at the palace, he played with the royal family, entertaining the children with stories of the Klondike, singing gold rush songs, and reciting the poems of Robert Service.

But Joe's short periods of leisure were not restful. He relentlessly continued his private war, and on June 18, while on one of his spy networking trips, he suffered a stroke in his hotel room in Kishinev (now Chisinau, Moldova). He was 50 years old. After his collapse, he was rushed to the city's Red Cross hospital. When Queen Marie was notified she sent her personal physician to Joe's aid. Strangely, and probably because of the chaotic status of the communications network, no word was sent home. While Marie knew about Joe's ex-wife Millie, she didn't know he had remarried so no official notice of his condition was sent to Elma. Joe's second marriage was a secret that would come to poison his relationship with Marie later.

"I felt my heart die within me," Marie wrote when she learned the news.

Joe's life lay in the balance for two weeks. He found himself alone in Bessarabia, his right side paralysed. Doctors told him any hope of being whole again was utterly impossible. But the doctors didn't know Joe Boyle. He faced this new personal challenge with as much stubborn will as he had any other. He spent hour after hour doing exercises before a mirror trying to regain the musculature on the stricken side of his face. It was a difficult and soul weary time for him.

Marie, terribly worried and unable to travel to

Bessarabia, ordered that he be moved to the summer palace in Bikaz where she said she intended to care for him personally. Joe, however, balked at this sympathy. He agreed to go only when she was willing to assign a peasant's cottage near the palace for his convalescence.

Marie personally supervised the preparations of the cottage, turning it into a most comfortable accommodation. Unable to be moved until the end of July, Joe was relocated to the Carpathian Mountains on August 1. Marie was there with young Princess Ileana to meet him when he arrived in the care of the British area commander General Ballard and the Rumanian ambassador to the court of St. James, Nicholas Misu.

The queen found Joe had regained his speech, and her patient was delighted to find Marie a loving attendant. During his convalescence he was free to spend an unrestricted amount of time with the woman he'd grown to love so deeply.

Yet Marie noticed the stroke had changed Joe in ways other than physical. "A certain sadness has crept into his being," she later wrote in her diary. "I feel that he knows he will never be quite the same again, and this is terrible to him." She redoubled her efforts to bring him back to his old vigorous self.

The queen, normally candid about her activities in her diary, was unusually discreet about Joe and the amount of time they spent in privacy. Each day they had breakfast together and when the weather allowed she took him on picnics.

The Canadian seemed to find new strength from this, and occasionally even welcomed visits from young Russian officers who delivered news about the ongoing struggles far beyond the quiet valley where he was recuperating. When Joe learned that the Russians had left 40 million lei (Rumanian currency) worth of medical supplies in Bessarabia, he was quick to convince Marie to buy this life-sustaining treasure for her people and to form a Red Cross mission that she could direct herself.

To get the purchase started, Joe contributed one million Lei of his own money. The selfless gesture touched Marie and she awarded him another medal, the Regina Maria, First Class, in gratitude.

"What I have felt about him is one of the good things of my life," she wrote. "He has been a lonely man and it seems incredible to him that the only woman he should finally have found as companion and co-worker should be a Queen."

Joe's close relationship with Marie extended to becoming part of the family in the royal household. On August 31, Marie tearfully told Joe that Prince Carol, her eldest son and heir apparent, had eloped to Odessa. Carol had long been at odds with Marie, refusing to

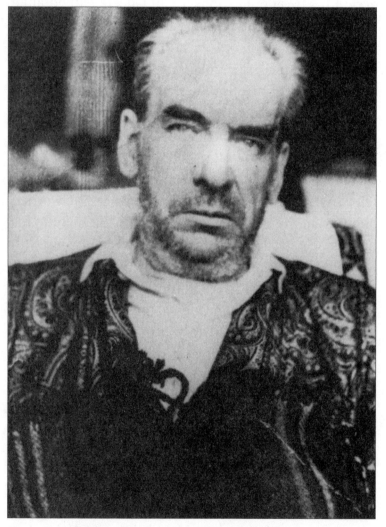

Recovering from a stroke, Kishinev 1918

accept his royal obligations. In an Odessa cathedral he had married Zizi Lambrinos, the daughter of a high-ranking Rumanian officer and a commoner. Marie asked Joe to speak to Carol on her behalf as "Uncle Joe," and convince him of the serious implications such a scandalous marriage would have on the royal family.

While he thanked Joe, King Ferdinand was hurt by Marie's personal request of the Canadian. In her diary, the queen didn't make any bones of the trepidation she felt when Ferdinand and Joe were together. She worried about what the king might do to rectify the slight to his honour, especially if he suspected her relationship with Joe was anything more than regal kindness. Nonetheless, Joe had several meetings with Carol, and during one discussion in Odessa, the prince threatened suicide if he was forced to return home without his bride. Recognizing the threat as mere drama, Joe calmly handed the prince his loaded revolver. Carol relented. The marriage was annulled and the prince returned home.

While Marie gushed with compliments for Joe, she harboured less enthusiasm for her husband. "Alas kings are not brought up to be men and I am afraid it is rather late to try to make a man out of Nando now that he is 53."

A few days before Joe's 51st birthday on November 6, 1918, Marie asked another favour of her champion. In late October 1918, the Bolsheviks announced that the Russian tsar had been executed on July 16. Would it be long before the rest of the family followed him to the grave? Marie asked Joe to perform his miracles. She wanted him to spirit her Aunt Minnie, the Russian Dowager Empress Marie Feodorovna, out of Crimea before the Bolsheviks decided to murder her as well.

Though he was far from recovered, Joe agreed to try. His spy network had reported to him that there was "a deliberate plot to kill the members of the royal family residing in the Crimea" when the Bolsheviks took over the Ukraine. After celebrating Armistice Day on November 11 with Queen Marie, her two eldest daughters, General Bailiff (Marie's aid), and General Ballard at the British Embassy, Joe left on the dangerous mission.

King Ferdinand granted him the command of a ship heading to the Crimea, and a detachment of 200 soldiers that Joe personally picked and outfitted with machine guns.

The Dowager Empress was living in her exposed summer palace compound not far from Yalta, about 90 kilometres from Sebastopol. Occupants of the palace consisted of the Dowager Empress; Grand Duke Nicholas and his family; Duchess Zenia, the eldest sister of the tsar, her husband Grand Duke Alexander and their family; and the Grand Duchess Olga, younger sister of the tsar.

Braving mines in the Black Sea, Joe arrived in Odessa on November 17. The occupying Germans showed little interest in the ship or its party, busy as they were with their own preparations to leave. The Bolsheviks were waiting for that moment and threatened to take over the ship. Joe tried to bluff them by keeping his ship's guns manned, but finally decided an old game of host was the best ploy.

Inviting them aboard he organized a huge party, and while they were being fed and entertained, he headed off alone to locate the Dowager Empress. He found her in her villa, but she refused to believe that her son had been murdered and therefore saw no need to leave. Joe provided what evidence he could with letters from Marie and Ferdinand. Marie Feodorovna still refused. She didn't fear the Bolsheviks, she said, and besides, the area was in the throes of an influenza epidemic. No one felt safe moving about in public inviting infection. Two naval destroyers, one British and one French, were on their way to Yalta, she told him. They could provide ample protection.

Joe had to concede, and promised to return in 24 hours in the event she changed her mind. When he did, he found "Aunt Minny" had prepared private letters she wished him to deliver personally to her sister, the Dowager Queen Alexandra in England, and to

King Ferdinand in Rumania.

He travelled back to Bucharest and the Cotroceni Palace, where Marie and Nando had moved in his absence, and delivered the letter to Ferdinand. Before leaving for England with his other private message for Queen Alexandra, Joe received the Croix de Guerre from France's General Berthelot. It meant he'd been decorated for valour by three nations, but still not his own. And he received something else from Marie.

A sizable ducal estate in Bessarabia was conferred upon him along with the royal title of Duke of Jassy in the Kingdom of Rumania. (When news of the title reached Canada the newspaper in Toronto ran an article asking "Is Elma Boyle the Duchess of Dawson?" and a clipping found its way to Marie.)

Joe met with Marie in her private quarters and urged her to send the best ship the Rumanian navy could find to England. Since he was going to London, he may as well perform a most necessary mission on behalf of Rumania. If she sent a ship, he pledged to fill it with supplies, saying he would somehow convince Herbert Hoover, then the head of the American Red Cross, to buy the goods Rumania needed.

Ecstatic at the prospects, Marie happily agreed to do as her not completely forthright champion asked. While he was going would he do another favour for the royal family? Her youngest son Prince "Nicky" was approaching an age of rebellion and neither she nor her milquetoast husband were able to control him. Could he take this feisty, fussing, and overindulged boy and deposit him at the Court of St. James where he could receive a stiff British education at Eton?

It hardly seemed an unusual request to Joe, who by now shared the queen's affections almost openly. He agreed to the assignment, taking the Rumanian ambassador along as a babysitter.

En route, Joe stopped in Paris, where the Versailles peace conference was to take place, and Misu parted company. Joe met with Herbert Hoover who was just installed in the American Relief Administration offices in the French capital, and then carried on to London, arriving on December 24, 1918. Nicky had become ill on the journey, but the following day he and Joe were presented to the British royal family at Buckingham Palace.

Afterwards, Joe wrote to Marie to report on the delivery of his precious cargo. On arrival at Buckingham Palace, he said he'd sent Nicky straight in to the king and queen and then waited for a half hour in the outer rooms before being granted his own audience. He met King George V and Queen Mary, as well as Princess Mary, Prince Henry, and Prince George. He told Marie he talked with the king for more than an hour, and made it clear that Marie most definitely wanted her 15-year-old son to receive a proper English education. Joe also supplied the king with details about the economic conditions in Rumania and Prince Carol's romantic episode.

While Joe was careful to be prompt in his note to Marie, he didn't bother to notify his family and friends in Canada that he was alive and well. He was probably utterly focussed on the now all-consuming love of his life, Queen Marie.

The Canadian government, however, managed to steal some of his attention. Canadian Prime Minister Sir Robert Borden got Joe to meet with him at Claridge's Hotel in London on the evening of December 29, 1918. Borden wanted to get Joe's personal opinion about the situation in Russia, and Joe provided it with both barrels. "Russia should be taken," he told the prime minister.

Borden's memoirs record Joe saying, "triumph of Bolshevism in Russia means that it will overrun Germany and that Germany and Russia will overrun the world or reduce organized society to anarchy. He insists that it must be put down … and declares that an army of a million men can do it. He says it will be a fraud and a sham if the Peace Conference concludes its labours without terminating the war and that cannot be done until anarchy is ended in Russia."

Joe, who continued to swagger in his honorary colonel's uniform, also asked for his rank to be regularized. He wasn't taken seriously even though he now had the ear of King George V. But the Canadian military simply didn't see him as part of their machine because he refused to take orders from anyone. Instead, they again demanded that he relinquish his uniform and stop using his honorary rank. Joe had learned about diplomacy in the year spent on the political knife-edge in Russia. He requested politely to be allowed to wear the uniform, as it represented an important symbol, whether real or perceived, in culturally backward Rumania. Without it, he said he felt he couldn't continue to perform the work he believed he could still complete.

No, they replied. That is precisely why it should be removed.

Joe dutifully switched to his civvies, but also promptly requested an audience with the king. When King George V was told why Joe was dressed in a suit, the sovereign commanded Joe put his uniform back on and told him to be confident in wearing army attire wherever and whenever he wished.

Driven about London in a limousine by young Prince Nicky, Joe managed, as the official representative of Rumania, to organize considerable relief for Queen Marie's country. It included nine cargo vessels for food and $25 million in loans from Canada for aid supplies.

Meanwhile, the Canadian military was still sniping. The king had settled the issue of the uniform, but it was up to them to decide if Joe should be regularized.

Colonel Pope supplied a telling report that ended the military's consideration. It was riddled with falsehoods.

"…the War Office makes certain strong allegations against Col. Boyle … that the man is a bluffing adventurer who knows how to make the most of his chances and should not receive official encouragement … What he did in Russia is unknown, but in due course he found his way to Rumania where he ingratiated himself with the Royal Family…. The Rumanian legation, from which he borrowed £100, dislike him strongly and their feelings were not softened when he produced a parchment, apparently faked in Canada, conferring a Rumanian "Dukedom" upon himself. There are certain outstanding law suits against Col. Boyle and it would appear inadvisable that he should be granted military status…"

Thumbing his nose at the military establishment, Joe headed to Paris to participate in the Versailles peace conference, all his medals clanging on his chest. There, rather than receiving support from the Rumanian government for his relief effort, he encountered his old rival, Ion C. Bratiano, who was again the Rumanian prime minister and who refused to recognize his credentials. Bratiano even attempted to publicly embarrass Joe in front of Hoover and others.

Joe tried to ignore Bratiano and requested a second meeting with Borden, who by now was joined by Sir Clifford Sifton, the chairman of the War Committee in Paris. Joe wanted to thank Borden for the aid package and press his opinion about Russia. Sifton listened politely and then told Joe he had a "fertile imagination" when it came to the Bolsheviks.

Not so at all, Joe replied. The danger was present and growing, he told them, and he requested Borden assign a contingent of 250 men to help the Rumanians reorganize their military in preparation for another onslaught by Russia. Borden told the Yukoner "there was no probability we would entertain any such proposal."

Perhaps feeling tired, ill, and alone among enemies, Joe contacted Marie to suggest she and Ferdinand attend the peace conference to ask for aid themselves. The government sent Marie. She was a tremendous weapon, as Joe had expected. He returned to London to tie up loose ends and the two were reunited in mid-March 1919.

The Rumanian queen arrived together with Princess Ileana. Marie had breakfast meetings with Joe at Buckingham Palace as the two conferred about what she might pursue at the Paris conference. When she returned to the conference, Joe stayed at Buckingham Palace to care for Ileana, who had fallen ill during the journey.

In Queen Marie's diaries, she wrote in familiar terms about how Joe had performed exceptional personal service for her. "He had seen everybody I wanted to hear about, had even run to Zurich to see my sister [Beatrice] and Ali [Beatrice's husband, Alfonso of Orleans-Bourbon]..."

Perhaps it was the familiarity Joe had gained with the royals of Europe that so perplexed and worried the British diplomats and the Canadian military. High-ranking officials seemed to be working in concert to try and build a better character profile on this enigmatic man because his secret exploits were still not known.

In spite of the military's efforts to officially dismiss him, Joe's "unofficial" status was quietly changed as far as the British were concerned in June 1919, when he was awarded the Distinguished Service Order (DSO) in the king's Birthday Honours List. Had Marie asked for George V's intervention in the matter, knowing how deeply Joe cared for his recognition as an officer? The DSO was awarded to officers who had performed meritorious or distinguished service in war. The decoration must have truly vexed the officials in the Foreign Office at Whitehall, who'd been trying to tame Joe for years, for the badge of the order, with its white and gold cross and red centre bearing a crown surrounded by a laurel wreath, showed their king had a differing opinion of the man.

After the Paris conference, Joe returned to Rumania with Marie, ostensibly in charge of the distribution of the supplies that Canada had so generously purchased. Joe, the man Marie called her "faithful backwoodsman" also put his mind to getting Rumanian oil resources back on stream.

Joe, it was reported by an aide sent to work with him for three years, had incredible authority once he returned. Lieutenant-Colonel Frank A. Reid later reported that he was "dumbfounded at the power Boyle wielded. It was unrestricted, his influence unlimited. He had complete control of all the secret police and he was a dictator, not only politically but also throughout the entire country, and as the country was full of intrigue he had an extremely busy time. We had secret agents working throughout the Russian oil fields and also agents throughout Rumania. Boyle's position as Red Cross commissioner was a clever cover-up."

According to Reid, Joe "was responsible for the law that enabled the peasant to buy land from the proprietor-landlord." He said Joe advocated expropriation of large landed estates for distribution to all deserving citizens. He wanted to see the entire population enfranchised. And through all he did, Joe maintained his secret network of spies who reported on the Bolshevik agitators. It was, for a time, the only reliable intelligence network in southern Russia.

But Joe's actions — his meddling in Rumania's internal affairs and his staunch support of Marie's efforts to improve conditions in her country — began to build a backlash both at court among the privileged and within the country's political ranks. Scandal-mongering newspapers criticized the "Saviour of Rumania" with relish, describing his openly romantic conduct with the queen, even claiming he'd been caught leaving her chamber half-dressed. As the pressure on her increased, Marie was finally forced to bend to the will of her advisors and the political leaders. She asked Joe to leave the country.

"After having made a hero out of him, almost a demi-god, they set upon him later, trying to blemish his honor, to pull him down, only because I knew he was big and trusted in him beyond what others considered it was wise to trust a man and especially a stranger. So they had to take him from me. I fought hard but finally had to surrender," Marie wrote later.

The Canadian left without an argument, and he

sent a short note to Marie. "I want you to be happy," he wrote. "That's all I know these days."

Chapter 8
The Legend Passes

Joe left Rumania but he didn't retire. He accepted a job with the oil company Royal Dutch-Shell, in Russia, and tried to use his connections to repatriate oil concessions that the Bolsheviks had cancelled. But his health began to fail rapidly. A deteriorating heart condition, complicated by kidney problems, weakened him dramatically. He struggled to win the concessions for his employers at an international economic conference in Genoa, but he was mostly confined to his bed or a wheelchair.

The burly man had withered. His weight slipped by 55 pounds and he looked gaunt. He went to London in early November 1923 to rest and recuperate and moved into a room supplied by his old Yukon friend, Teddy Bredenberg. He knew he was slipping away, but refused to complain even when Royal Dutch-Shell fired him. Because his condition made writing nearly impossible, Tony Bredenberg, Teddy's son, helped him compose several letters to Marie. He did manage to write two letters himself, which he slipped under his pillow on April 13, 1923.

That night, Joe didn't sleep. By 10 a.m. the next morning, as the curtains were being opened so he might catch a glimpse of the sunlight on the spire of St. James' Church across the road, he died silently.

Teddy Bredenberg discovered Joe's hidden letters. One was addressed to him and expressed Joe's gratitude for his friendship. The other was to Queen Marie. Bredenberg mailed Joe's last private note to Marie that morning. He telegrammed Queen Marie to express brief sympathy and then contacted Joe Jr. The young Boyle happened to be in London, but he had barely made time for his father in the final days. When informed of his father's death, Joe Jr. told Bredenberg to make any funeral arrangements he wanted. Joe's son said it would be unnecessary for him to come before the funeral on April 16.

An aide named Tzegintzov, who had helped Joe for

years in his Russian escapades, took time to write to Queen Marie with full details of Joe's death. She replied to Tzegintzov with a 12-page note that said, without doubt, how much she loved Joe.

No one knew his heart better than I…. He did not believe in dreams, was furious at the dreamy…and yet when one comes to consider his life, he was always led by dreams — by impossible dreams of a world in which men could play fair and fight fair, help each other and speak the truth — dreams…there was not a week that I did not write to him, did not make a report of my doings. I kept him in touch with every event of our lives…. For us he is not dead, he was so big, he is in the trees, in the sky, in the sea, in the sun and the wind…he is in the freshness of early morning and the silence of the night — and the stars seem to watch me with his eyes and the clouds seem to bring me messages from that great heart that was mine….

Marie couldn't attend Joe's funeral, and in her place a spray of orange lilies, flowers that the couple used as a private signal of love, were placed on his grave.

Months later, Queen Marie arrived to spend some

Joe Boyle's grave in Woodstock, Ontario

time in the room where Joe had died. Bredenberg left her in privacy for a long time while she wept. Marie had a slab, shipped from Rumania, placed over his grave. She sent an ancient stone cross and urn for flowers. She personally planted tendrils of ivy that she had carried from her palace garden around the headstone.

Every year, until Marie died just before the start of World War II, a woman in black appeared at Joe's grave with orange lilies. The woman would carefully prune the ivy and kneel at the grave, weeping.

Epilogue

For many years, very little was known about Joe's true exploits. To the astonishment of his compatriots, publicly and in secret, he had fought his nation's adversaries with courage and daring.

Joe so often succeeded through his force of character where lesser men refused to try. He maintained a common touch with everyone, which made him friends among his staunchest business enemies and earned him the awe of his political foes.

He had magnificent faults, as has any great man with an impetuous nature, and he accomplished magnificent things in spite of them. Joe turned from almost every personal relationship he'd ever had except for one. That love, a love he could never completely own, he cherished to his last breath.

It took 60 years before the Royal Canadian Legion in Joe's hometown of Woodstock repatriated the hero's body on April 20, 1983. The effort was a testament of honour for a man who so richly deserved recognition in his own country. He rests in Woodstock now on a hillside, never having felt the glow of pride to be had from a simple thanks offered by his homeland.

Klondike Joe Boyle is an unsung national hero. Perhaps someday, a mute nation will recognize him with a stamp, his etched image in full dress uniform.

Joe might have liked that.

Military Orders and Awards received by Lieutenant Colonel Joseph Whiteside Boyle, DSO
• Distinguished Service Order — England
• Croix de Guerre — France
• Order of the Star of Romania (Grand Cross) — Romania
• Order of the Crown of Romania (Commander) — Romania
• Order of Regina Maria — Romania
• Order of St. Vladimir, 4th Class — Russia
• Order of St. Anne, 4th Class — Russia
• Order of St. Stanislaus, 2nd Class — Russia

Source: Official military records in Ottawa

Bibliography

Berton, Pierre. *Klondike*. Toronto: McClelland & Stewart, 1963.

Berton, Pierre. *The Klondike Quest: A Photographic Essay,* 1879-1899. Toronto: McClelland & Stewart, 1983.

Berton, Pierre. *The Wild Frontier.* Toronto: McClelland & Stewart, 1982.

Black, Martha Louise. *My Ninety Years.* Ed. Flo Whyard. Anchorage: Alaska Northwest Publishing Co., 1976.

Boyle, Flora Alexander. "Who Was Joe Boyle?" Toronto: *MacLean's Magazine,* 1938.

Elsberry, Terence. *Marie of Romania.* New York: St. Martin's Press, 1972.

Foote, Isabel. *In Praise of a Canadian Hero.* Woodstock: Oxford Historical Society, 1997.

Bibliography

Palmer, R.R., Joel G. Colton, & Lloyd S Kramer. *A History of the Modern World,* Toronto: McGraw Hill College Division, 2001.

Rodney, William. *Joe Boyle, King of the Klondike.* Toronto: McGraw-Hill Ryerson Ltd., 1974.

Taylor, Leonard W. *The Sourdough & The Queen.* Toronto: Metheun, 1983.

Acknowledgments

The author would like to acknowledge the superb research in two previously published works by authors Leonard W. Taylor and William Rodney. The books provided a colourful tapestry of facts from which I was able to draw for this short tribute to the life of Joe Whiteside Boyle.

Photograph Credits

About the Author

Stan Sauerwein lives and writes in Westbank, British Columbia. A freelance writer for two decades, his articles have appeared in a variety of Canadian and U.S. magazines and newspapers. Specializing in business subjects, he has written for both corporations and governments. He is the author of three other books — *Rattenbury: The Life and Tragic End of B.C.'s Greatest Architect; Ma Murray: The Story of Canada's Crusty Queen of Publishing;* and *Fintry: Lives, Loves and Dreams.*

OTHER AMAZING STORIES

These titles are available wherever you buy books. If you have trouble finding the book you want, call the Altitude order desk at 1-800-957-6888, e-mail your request to: orderdesk@altitudepublishing.com or visit our Web site at www.amazingstories.ca

All titles retail for $9.95 Cdn or $7.95 US. (Prices subject to change.)

New AMAZING STORIES titles are published every month. If you would like more information, e-mail your name and mailing address to: amazingstories@altitudepublishing.com.